The Heart of
A Man
by
Oscar J. Peskoff

iUniverse, Inc.
Bloomington

The Heart of a Man
One World, One People

iUniverse books may be ordered through booksellers or by contacting:

*iUniverse
1663 Liberty Drive
Bloomington, IN 47403
www.iuniverse.com
1-800-Authors (1-800-288-4677)*

*Because of the dynamic nature of the Internet, any web addresses or links contained in this book may
have changed since publication and may no longer be valid.*

*Any people depicted in stock imagery provided by Thinkstock are models,
and such images are being used for illustrative purposes only.*

Certain stock imagery © Thinkstock.

*ISBN: 978-1-4620-1415-6 (sc)
ISBN: 978-1-4620-1417-0 (dj)
ISBN: 978-1-4620-1416-3 (ebk)*

Printed in the United States of America

iUniverse rev. date: 4/21/2011

PROLOGUE

E very life story has a start, which begins at birth. Throughout the years that follow, there are many events that occur and can be categorized as happy times and sad times with many ups and downs, such as you find on a roller coaster ride at an amusement park. All of these events are catalogued in your mind, not necessarily in chronological order. However, they are remembered in their proper time frame, and they are etched in the brain memory center. Many of these little episodes are very meaningful, and have been part of what I consider a very happy and fulfilling life. They have all contributed to my education and have given me the confidence to attempt this literary effort.

If you have good recall and are mentally alert, you can bring each of these memories into focus and bring them back and relive each and every one of them and put them into words. You will remember that some of them were glad, some were sad, and then there were the ones that you wish didn't happen. None of these events can be erased from your memory and until you forget, they will be etched in your mind forever.

When an inexperienced writer attempts to relive his life as I am doing with this effort, it is inevitable that times and places may not be in their proper sequence. So it is with this story, which is about to unfold. This is not a biography. Biographical stories have a set pattern in that they begin at birth, a pattern of life experiences occurs, and it ends, every time, with death.

This story is different, in that it is autobiographical, and I consider it a work in progress.

I give credit to my wife, Sharry, for giving me the inspiration to attempt this project, and I thank her and my daughter, Ellen, for their editorial assistance and support for my efforts. This book is dedicated to them for their believing that I could undertake and complete this momentous undertaking.

Let me begin these pages of my life with the three words that start the first page of the Old Testament.

In the beginning.......

MY STORY

OSCAR J. PESKOFF

CHAPTER I

I was born on June 16th 1920, in Bensonhurst, Brooklyn, N.Y. My parents, Morris and Bessie Peskoff, like so many of their generation, fled the pogroms of Russia/Poland, and sailed to the United States in search of a safer and more promising life. My Mom used to tell me stories about how I was delivered at home for 50 cents. That is how it was in those days.

I was the 2nd of four children. My brother Simon was 2 years older, and my younger siblings were twins, Herbert and Shirley, who were 4 years younger. Needless to say, the only girl child, Shirley got most of the attention.

While I was growing up, my mother was the primary influence in my life. She taught me to be charitable, to be kind, and to be a gentleman. When I came home with bruises and scratches, she would clean me up, apply a bandage, kiss me and tell me I would be fine, and to go outside and play. I remember my mother with the fondest and loving memories, and I believe that she was largely responsible for my being the man I am today.

The first story of my youth is unforgettable. When I was born, we lived in an apartment over a storefront on 19th Avenue just off Bath Avenue. Solomon the Glazier had his business in a shop just below our front windows. I was about 4, Simon was 6, and the twins were tiny. Simon had a puppy to play with, and he wouldn't let me pet the dog. I was angry and wanted revenge, so I opened the front window, and tossed the puppy out into the street. He dropped about 8 feet and landed in the padded cart that the glazier used to make deliveries. It was miraculous because the puppy wasn't injured. Needless to say, I was punished. I was hurting and crying, and as mad as I could be. I was mad at my mother, and wanted to respond, so I found some matches and torched her celluloid dresser set. The flames were fast and smoky, and the prompt fire department response kept the damage to the dresser top. The end result to this episode was another spanking, a puppy recovered unhurt, and my first nickname, "fireman", which stayed with me until we moved from this apartment into a four family house, which my Grandpa Sam bought for my mother.

Like all kids growing up in Brooklyn in the 20's and 30's, we got into the usual mischief that boys got into, nothing serious, but just enough to get us a few laughs now and then. For instance, on an occasional Monday evening, around 8 PM, my gang would go to the local J.C.H., which was a focal point in our Community, and peek through the tilted window, into the girls' locker room. Being the shortest in my gang, I got to be the lowest head at the window. I was being picked on now and then, for being such a runt. Peeking in at the women who were not always dressed, was exciting, and a different experience for us. Sometimes, Being short had its benefits. With my mothers' guidance, I learned how to handle most of the situations, and eventually earned the respect of my friends.

My father was born in what was then called Russia/Poland. His father William had 5 children with his first wife. When she died, he married a cousin from his wife's family and fathered four additional children. My dad was the first of these 4 children. Then the exodus began, and the Peskofsky family started across the Atlantic and settled on Henry Street in lower Manhattan. My grandfather became the "Shamus" in the local synagogue and made arrangements to bring the family over. I don't know how long it took, but his mission was accomplished, successfully. The family was intact and began a new life.

My father was a very lucky man, and although he had no real education, he learned to write his name, and read the daily papers. His greatest interest was figuring the daily numbers, which were gleaned from the results of the daily race results. That, and playing "pinochle" at the rear of the local delicatessen were his main activities after work. He also ventured out on an occasional Sunday afternoon, and watched semi-pro baseball at a local baseball field. His main interest at home, was sitting in front of the TV set, in his armchair, with a bottle of beer, and watch wrestling. The rest of his family activities were arranged by my mother, who made all of the plans.

Like other men of my father's generation, he only knew that he had to work hard and earn a living to support his family, and he was a very diligent worker. He had a change in direction when his friend Ed Peckelis was drafted into the Army. He offered my father the laundry wagon, and told him to take over his wet wash route. He left the slaughterhouse, and became an independent worker. After the war was over, and Ed Peckelis returned, they realized that there was enough business for both of them to earn a living. This was the beginning of a partnership that lasted over 50 years. It started with a handshake, and ended with a handshake, when Ed and his wife Edna moved to Florida. Our families remained friends until Ed and Edna passed away.

When the laundry wagon pickups were decreasing, it became evident that their partnership had to make some new decisions. They were approached by two cousins who worked in the laundry processing the wet wash, with a proposition to join them in a laundry venture of their own. Lou Maslow and Irving Mosler wanted to open their own laundry and needed $4000 dollars to go into business. Each would put in an equal share. The end result was that my father didn't want to think positive, and the arrangement was cancelled. However, my dad and Ed loaned them the $2000 dollars, so that they could go ahead with their plans. That was my fathers' 1st missed Golden Opportunity. Today, that little venture has grown into what is now the Consolidated Laundries, Inc., which is a multi-million dollar corporation.

His friendship with Ed Peckelis was the best thing that happened to him. I should say 2nd best, because he chased my mother, who lived across the Brooklyn Bridge, in Brooklyn, and finally wore her resistance down. After they were married, my father changed his name from Peskofsky to Peskoff. My mom was named Bessie, one of eight Friedman children. My father, as I said before, was a very lucky man. His friendship with Ed Peckelis was unbelievable and unimaginable. If I tell you that my father could have been a very wealthy man, I am not telling you a lie. He chose not to open his own laundry business, which was his first missed opportunity. Little did he realize that this was the first of his many negative decisions.

Grandpa Sam Friedman had a different life before he came to the United States. Here, he managed to keep himself busy with his needle and sewing talents, and managed to raise the family successfully. In Russia, he was in the Army, and was a tailor for the Czar in the Kremlin. He made uniforms for the Officers, and was very ingenious, because he arranged for female companionship for the Officers whenever there were parties at the Palace. He was a very valuable asset, and got many favors for himself. He had many furloughs, and got to see his family on a regular basis. He was very prolific and was the father of 8 children, five girls and 3 boys. His talents included sewing and "sowing", and he was good at both efforts. My cousin Kay always told us stories of Grandpa Sam, the pimp for the Czar.

CHAPTER II

The partnership decided to enter into a new venture, and began processing raw alcohol into bootleg scotch. They combined alcohol, distilled water, coloring and blended the concoction with real Johnny Walker Scotch. They operated a still in Brooklyn and set up malt and hops shops in Brooklyn and Manhattan. It was a very successful operation, and the locations were all doing a good business. During prohibition, malt and hops sales were not illegal, and the storefronts operated with those two products for sale. There was no visual activity with the alcohol end of the operation.

In all fairness, this illegal operation, such as it was, produced a very fine and acceptable product. Sales and distribution were more than adequate, and a third partner was brought into the operation. His name was Ralph Barry, and he became another "uncle". He joined the partnership with a handshake. There were many days after school when I would walk up to the shop off 18th Avenue and help put labels on the bottles. In those days, we didn't have glue- ons, so we had to wipe the glue side and apply it to the bottles. It was a time consuming process, and getting paid was a real plus.

I remember on a few occasions that my father took me on delivery trips with him. Dad drove a four door "hupmobile" sedan, which had a false bed under the floor boards. They would load about 20 cases of the bootleg Johnny Walker Scotch underneath, and off we would go to the Boston area. His contact in that area was Joseph Kennedy, who supposedly ran the bootleg operation in the New England area. Little did we know that he would be the father of John Kennedy, who was to be the President of the United States.

What my father was doing was illegal, and I didn't know it at the time. Dad came home at night and emptied his pockets into Mom's apron, as she was the custodian of the cash. Because of his line of work, our family did not suffer from the depression. In fact, my dad was very generous in the community. He would lend money to those who needed it and never charge any interest. My dad was a religious man, and charging interest wasn't in his nature. Many of those loans were never repaid, and my father didn't care. He used to say, "as long as we have enough, it doesn't matter". I learned that trait from my dad. Money is only a commodity to be used judiciously, and not to be wasted. Enjoying the fruits of my labor, has been a part of my life, and it has worked very well over all of these years.

When repeal was enacted, the partnership was offered an opportunity to get legal liquor store licenses for each of the Malt and Hop shops. The partners huddled, and, in his inimitable fashion, my dad said, "I DON'T NEED IT". That ended the discussion, and Golden Opportunity # 2 went by with no thoughts of the future.

My dad, and his partners, had many friends from many walks of life: including politicians, local officials, and other hard working entrepreneurs. They all respected the integrity of the product, and the honesty of the men who were delivering the goods. No one ever complained about getting any bad products. My dad was so well respected, that when I was bar mitzvahed, he invited many of his customers to attend the festivities. The ballroom in Brooklyn was large enough to accommodate a large crowd, and when they were all seated, I looked down from the platform and saw the alignment. My family was in the center section, the local officials were on the right side, and the hard working entrepreneurs were on the left side. I delivered my speech in Yiddish, which was important, because many of my family, in particular my grandpa Sam, couldn't understand English too well. It was a very successful presentation, and I was very happy that it went off so well. The evening went very well, as planned, with lots of good food, plenty of good drink, and lots of music and happy activity. This was 1933, and it was customary to give gifts, which included $20 dollar gold coins. Just visualize me, in my blue serge suit, loading my pockets with the gift envelopes. I was walking off balance after a while. It was my day to shine, and I recall the events with happy memories.

When I was around 10 or 11, I had a good friend, who was the brother of Sophie Tuckers's piano accompanist. I used to hang out at their house, across the street. They, of course, had a grand piano, and I, ever so gently, used to tickle the "ivories". His brother Ted Shapiro was listening to me one afternoon, and then asked me if I had a piano. I told him I didn't, and he said he liked the way I touched the keys. He was going to ask my mother to get me a piano, and he would give me lessons. After some discussion between my mom and dad, it was agreed that I would get the piano, and so, my lessons began. I was an eager and willing student, and I was progressing very rapidly. By the time I was 14, I was playing the first 14 bars of the Beethoven "Moonlight Sonata". Of course, about that time I had discovered that there were girls in this world, and that was pretty much the end of my piano playing for the time being. The next time I touched a piano was when I was in the Armed Services, with the 5th Air Force in Australia, and found a piano in the PX at our station. But that's another story for later.

I was ambitious, and eager to get out there and be a part of the world. I even got myself a job, after school, working at the corner grocery store, delivering orders. I sat on an empty milk crate in front of the store, and waited for the owner to call me to deliver a package for one of the customers, who couldn't carry the bag home. I got paid 5 cents for each delivery, and had a sheet at the register, marking each delivery. I was paid every Friday afternoon. There weren't that many deliveries, and just sitting out front became a little boring. So, I occasionally went into the store and picked up a package of chocolate icing covered cupcakes, and slowly nibbled on them to pass the time. I made a mark on the pay sheet every time I took another package. By the time Friday came around, and we balanced my earnings against my spending, it usually worked out even. I didn't mind going home broke. I was satisfied that I kept busy and was doing something constructive. Mom didn't mind either because I was keeping myself out of trouble.

Another flashback memory is very relevant. It was my custom to join my father at his synagogue for the high holiday services. He was an orthodox observer, and I shared the days of prayer with him and my grandfather Sam. In the old days it was the custom of the rabbi to raise funds by auctioning off the "aleyahs", and he would have the congregants bid for each honor. My father was a very active bidder, and managed to raise the bidding to generous amounts. In most cases he was the successful bidder, and he would then have the Rabbi give the honors to deserving congregants who could not be so generous. This was another way of my fathers showing his generosity to his neighbors and friends.

This "shul" was a storefront synagogue with pull chain lights throughout the building. Dad wanted to do something special for the Rabbi and asked me to go to the local hardware store and arrange for a fluorescent fixture to be installed wherever there was a pull chain light. My father would pay the bill. When I told the store owner the story, he told me that he would install the fixtures and ask my father just to pay for the fixtures. He would do the labor as a donation to the synagogue. This was a win win situation, and one of the many good things that my father did in his lifetime. This was his style. He did what he wanted to do because he could. This was his way of life. All I remember is that wherever I went, my father had been there before me.

CHAPTER III

Let me go back to my earlier years, when I was about 5 years old. It was on a regular visit to Grandma Friedman, on Madison Street in Manhattan. It was a snowy weekend, and I was outside playing in the snow, while the family was upstairs with Grandma. I was making a snowball, and unknowingly picked up a sliver of glass with the snow. In crunching the snow, the glass pierced my 4th finger on my right hand. I was bleeding and screaming, as I was running upstairs, clutching my finger. With experience of a true grandma, she cuddled me, and very simply pulled the glass from my finger. She washed away the blood and wrapped a clean piece of linen around my finger. Then, with a kiss and a hug, and a pat on my rear, she handed me a cookie, and said, "you're alright again. Now go out and play". I guess Tender Loving Care dates back to those years as well.

I still look at the scar on my finger, and recall kicks in. It is a wonderful recollection of such a lovely person. I guess all mothers and grandmothers, in those days, had the internal smarts for curing and protecting those that they were responsible for.

My mother inherited that same empathy. I recall, when I fell off the stoop and cracked my elbow, she rushed me to the doctor, and said, "you can cry; it helps heal the pain". It was a lesson well taught, because when I am a situation where there is sorrow, or something sad has happened, I get teary. When I had to make an announcement from the pulpit of our Synagogue, when I was the President, I started by brushing my nose. Congregants would say, "there he goes again; he's going to cry". That feeling is with me today, even at the movies, when something sad is happening, I get tears in my eyes.

I tell another story of my early years, when I was about 5 or 6 years old. It was a Sunday morning, and most families were at home preparing for their Sunday dinner, with the whole family at the table. I heard a violin playing on the alley, and saw my mother wrapping a few pennies in brown paper, to throw out the window, to the man playing the violin .I asked her why she was throwing money down to the man, and she answered: "my son, that man is too proud to ask for charity, so he is using his talents to entertain. He is trying to please us with his music, in hopes that we will reward him with some money. He has pride, and would never ask for help. When you grow up, with situations such as this, put your hand in your pocket and take out a dollar. Give it as a gift, and when you put your hand back in your pocket, you will find another dollar. The fact that you give charity will make you a better person. I live that way, and I want you to live the same". That was a lesson I have never forgotten.

I must go back to my younger years, as a child on 85th Street in Bensonhurst. When we moved to the four family house that Grandpa Sam Friedman bought for my mom, I was about 5 years old. My elementary schooling was at P.S.128, which was around the corner, on 84th Street. It was during these years, as I was beginning to wonder about growing up and how my life was going to be, that I became very inquisitive. And, as I soon began to learn, my mom had most of the answers. She had all of my questions under control, and gave me all the answers. She was my problem solver, and nothing was left unresolved. I wrote elsewhere about my piano lessons. She solved that situation, by seeing to it that I had a piano. When I wanted to go ice skating with the older boys, way down on 86th Street, in Dyker Heights, mom got me ice skates and arranged for me to join the group.

The next Saturday morning, the gang arranged to go down to the Dyker Heights park and go ice skating. Mom packed me a lunch and gave me 15 cents for the day. Ten cents for the trolley round trip, and a nickel for candy at Woolworth's department store. Off I went, ready for a full day outdoors, with my brown bag in tow. We had a great time, and later in the afternoon, we left for the trip back to 21st Avenue and home. It was cold, and we were hungry and waiting at the trolley stop for the next trolley. Bauer's Bakery was at this corner, and we were getting the aroma of the fresh baked breads and rolls. We took a vote and had to make a choice. Do we buy rolls with the last nickels and walk home, or do we get on the trolley hungry? We decided to buy the freshly baked rolls, and each of us got the 4 rolls for a nickel, and we ate them on the long walk back home. That was the end of a very happy and eventful day.

When I was 11 or 12, Mom let me go up to the Bronx to see my Aunt Fannie and, Kay and Ida, my girl cousins. They lived in an apartment house on E 143rd Street. They also had a candy store, which was at the front entrance to the building. I loved going up there, on the free weekends, standing behind the counter and wrapping the pennies. And, not to forget to mention, dipping into the freezer box to pick up a frozen chocolate twist candy every once in a while. If you can imagine, going on the BMT subway, from 20th Avenue, all the way to 42nd Street, and then walking two long blocks to the 3rd Avenue El, for a ride through Manhattan, into the Bronx. The 143rd Street station was on the block where my Aunt had the store. I was an adventuresome kid, and with Moms' confidence in me, I was able to grow with a strong belief in myself.

CHAPTER IV

It was shortly after moving to 81ˢᵗ St., with grandpa Sam Friedman living with us, and everything was working very smoothly. Mom had finished decorating the new apartment and getting ready for the Thanksgiving holiday. Herb was working as a delivery boy for a fruit store, and he had just gotten a present of a live Albino turkey. He brought it home and gave it to my mother. This was going to be part of our Thanksgiving dinner on the following Thursday. Mom decided to keep the bird tied to the faucet in the bathtub. She didn't want it to be walking around the apartment.

When dad came home and saw the bird in the tub, he was shaken up. When he heard the whole story, he relaxed, and got to like the bird. He even washed his feathers every day, so that he would look clean and pretty. This was a daily ritual for him. The bird got a bath every night. Wednesday was decision day, and mom told Simon to take the bird to the butcher and have him slaughtered, and prepared for the dinner table. Simon completed the mission, and brought the prepared bird home for mom to put into the refrigerator until the following morning.

Thursday morning was a very busy time in our kitchen. The bird was in the oven, the brisket was on the stove, all the incidental stuff was being prepared, and we were getting the dinner table set for the family dinner. When dad came home, dinner was ready, and the seven of us gathered at the table. When it came to the main course, Mom brought in the brisket and then went out and brought in the turkey and put it down in front of my dad. He had the honor of carving the bird. I don't know how it happened, but no one was making a sound, and dad wasn't picking up the carving set. We all just sat there and stared at the bird. I guess it was mental telepathy, but mom realized that this wasn't going to be a part of our dinner. She just got up, picked up the platter, and brought it back into the kitchen. When she returned, she started serving the brisket and other stuff. Everyone relaxed and enjoyed the rest of the dinner. Grandpa Sam, who usually didn't talk very much, agreed that we did the right thing. The next morning, Simon took the uneaten bird to the YMCA, and gave it to the caretaker for their dinner.

While grandpa Sam was living with us on 81st Street mom fell ill and had to have an appendectomy operation. When she was hospitalized, we had to send Grandpa to a nursing home on a temporary basis. We made arrangements for Grandpa to be in a home in the neighborhood, and we brought him there. When he was settled in and unpacked, he asked me how long he would be there. I told him, and he said, "show me on the calendar". I marked the calendar, and left him. We figured it would be a week before Mom could be brought home, and all of us were comfortable with the arrangement. We brought Mom home after her successful surgery and recovery, and I called the Nursing home to tell them that I was coming for my Grandfather. The Office Manager told me that he was ready to go, and when I got there, I found him sitting on his bed, fully dressed and waiting for me. The nurse told me that he had his breakfast, and dressed himself, because the calendar said he was going home on that day. His first words were, translated from Yiddish, "Am I coming home now". Yes, he was coming home, to his own bedroom.

My mother's home was the meeting grounds for all of the families who lived in the area, and most every birthday party for the kids was celebrated there. The last party was Ellen's third birthday, and since I was the family photographer, I took all the movies of the birthday parties. As her cousin Steve was the oldest of the grandchildren, he always sat next to Ellen. When she blew out the candles, he was the first to kiss her on the cheek. As a matter of fact, they are still kissing cousins. Steve is in his sixties and Ellen is a few years back. They are still in touch and have developed a very fond relationship. Steve and Karen have two sons, Jeremy and Jonathan, and Jonathan's wife Marla is about to deliver their first grandchild. This baby will be the first girl child of this generation.

I remember when Steve was old enough, he would walk from Bay Parkway to 19th Avenue, and visit my mom and Grandpa Sam. He would bring his homework, visit with Grandpa and then go home after dinner.

Memories of these early years, when the kids were growing up, bring back little incidents that bear mention. When the house was too crowded, Dorothy and I would hide in the den, and snuggle on the couch. On one occasion, Steve came back and saw us, and then ran to grandma and said, "grandma, they're playing dirty".

Mom was very smart and always told him that married people always stayed close. She was also a talented diplomat in her quiet way. There was a time when Mom and Dad had a very important party to go to, and they didn't want Grandpa to stay alone, so they asked Dorothy to get permission to sleep at our house that night. Dorothy was to sleep with Mom in her bed, and Dad would sleep in the den with me.

When it was time for bed, Dorothy got into her pajamas, and was under the covers. I was still in my clothes, on top of the blanket, and we were snuggling. The next thing I remembered was my mother waking us up. Dorothy and I were both under the blanket, fast asleep. She told us that when she got home, we were both asleep, so she got me under the blanket and tucked me in also. When Dorothy got dressed she was embarrassed, and Mom brushed it off as a "nothing". and Dorothy was relaxed again.

There was an afternoon, when I took Steve and Grandpa Sam to 86th Street, to buy Grandpa a pair of shoes at Thom McCann. As we were about to leave the store with the new shoes, Grandpa said to me, "du hust meir gelt", meaning, do you have more money? I said yes and asked him, why? He said he wanted to buy "schtekschich", which means rubbers, so that he wouldn't wear out the new shoes too quickly. We went back into the store and bought the rubbers. This man was still sharp as a tack.

My only regret is that I never thought about taking the time to teach him to speak English. He could have told us all the stories about his time in the Russian Army, and the things he did at the Kremlin. As grandpa Sam aged, he grew mellow, and lived out the last years of his life with my Mom and Dad in Brooklyn. He had survived 3 heart attacks, and was slowing down considerably. He spent his days reading his prayer book, his hands quivering, but nonetheless, he managed to recite the words. I doubt that he was reading, because he must have memorized the scriptures over the years of constant praying. He treasured that book, and kept it at his side at all times. His Parkinson's tremor was always present, except when he was using a needle and thread. Then, his hand became as steady as an arrow, and the needlework was in a perfectly straight line. He could repair a patch in a plaid coat, and no one could see the repair work. He was the finest tailor I ever knew.

When he had his 4th heart attack at age 104, my mom said that she wouldn't let him go to the Hospital. She wanted him to stay at home, in his own bed, and we would bring the hospital here. We arranged for a hospital bed to be delivered, and hired nurses for around the clock duty. Everything that was needed to monitor his condition was on hand, and we settled in and were ready for any emergency.

I left instructions with the Nurses, to call me immediately if anything happened. I lived 10 minutes away, and would get there as soon as I could. Everything was going along with no problems for about a week, and then I got an emergency call around 3 AM one morning. The nurse was upset, and was telling me that my grandfather was having a tantrum. I got there in about 15 minutes, and found all the lights on in the apartment. I rushed into the bedroom and found my grandfather sitting in a chair next to his bed, the nurse was very upset, and saw that my grandfather was very agitated.

When I asked the nurse to tell me what had happened, she said that she was trying to hold my grandfather from climbing out of the bed, and he got very excited and yelled at her. My grandfather only spoke "Yiddish", so I realized that there was a lack of communication.

Then I went to my grandfather, and asked him what happened, he said, in "Yiddish", the "golem" thought I was climbing out of bed. I wasn't climbing out. I had to go to the bathroom, and she was sleeping, so I climbed over the rail and went to the bathroom. When I was trying to climb back in, she woke up and grabbed me. She couldn't understand me, and I couldn't understand her. What I was trying to say was, "I'M NOT CLIMBING OUT, I'M CLIMBING BACK". Peace and quiet was restored, and everyone settled down. I went home very relieved. Several days later, his life ended, quietly and in his sleep. He lived a full and prosperous life, and when he died, he still had a full set of teeth, a full head of hair and a manicured beard. When he left this world, at 104, he left a loving family that will always cherish his memory.

CHAPTER V

My father, unfortunately, had no vision of the future. All he knew was that he had to make a living, to provide for his family, and be kind to friends and neighbors. He was a good man, and he had good virtues. He was honest, trustworthy, friendly, curious and kind; and had all of the Boy Scout virtues. His devotion to work and providing for his family clouded out other important attributes. He loved his family in his own way, but he showed very little outward emotion. He never wanted or needed anything for himself. He was a man of few words. Most of them were NO, and YOU DON'T NEED IT!

He had enough and wanted to live a simple life. All he needed was a comfortable home, a relaxed evening in front of the TV watching his favorite wrestling programs, sitting in his favorite chair, with a bottle of beer in his hand. When he went out in the evening, it was to play pinochle at the neighborhood delicatessen, with his friends from the neighborhood. If the family had to go someplace, he was the chauffeur, and never complained about having to visit.

Dad enjoyed an occasional baseball game, at the local semi pro ball field, and he went with his friend, Pete Levy. If I was around when they were leaving, Pete insisted that I go along. It was a treat, and some days I came home with a free foul ball, which someone caught and gave to me. He let my Mom run the family and the household, and she was a great manager. Our home was the gathering place for the rest of the families in the clan. The Friedman clan were very close and compatible, and we were always visiting or being visited by them. We had a Friedman family circle, which met every few months. The usual attendance was about 30 people, including the kids, and we used a local meeting hall for the occasions.

My mother had a magic pot on the stove, and it was always simmering with "stuff". I never asked what was in it, but I always knew that it was going to be very tasty and palatable. Our home was like a hotel on the weekends. Company coming and going, and no one went away hungry. It was always a warm and loving get together. Mom was a great organizer.

I remember, when we were still living on 85th Street, my mother telling my dad, that when he came home tonight, we would be at a new address. She gave him a note with a new address, and said, "tonight, after work, you go to 1902 81st, Apartment A. We will be moving into that apartment during the day, and dinner will be there". He never said a word or asked a question. He must have thought, if it was good for Mom it would be good for him". And so it happened.

My brother Simon and I finally had a bedroom of our own, and we wouldn't have to open cots in the living room in order to get to sleep. The twins would have the second bedroom. My piano was the centerpiece in the new living room. Simon and I slept on a double sleeper couch, and it was finally a comfortable sleeping arrangement. We had all of the conveniences, including clothes closets that we could call our own. It was a real luxury after all these years. Our little puppy, "snooky" loved to sit at the piano bench and listen to me practice. Then when Simon took out his violin, the dog would start to howl and run into another room. I guess he didn't like the high notes on the violin.

I had just graduated from elementary school, and was accepted into James Madison High School. My grades at elementary were good, which gave me the option of picking my choice of High School rather than go to New Utrecht, which was just a few blocks away. My choice was easy, because I had a crush on a girl who was going there, and I wanted to be near her whenever I could. Hazel Weisbard was a very pretty girl, and she towered over me by 4 inches. She was kind and friendly, and let me carry her books to the bus stop. We walked from 19th Avenue to Bay Parkway, three long blocks, morning and afternoon. It was the same routine. I waited outside her house, and we walked to the bus together. It was a daily ritual until I got involved with the basketball team.

I was appointed an assistant manager, and my interests took a different tack. I would be having other responsibilities. I was too short to be competitive, but I wanted to be around the ballplayers, and I was appointed as an assistant manager. I guess I was beginning to look to the future, and starting to think about who I was, and what I wanted to become. In retrospect, Hazel was my first female friend. I never even got to hold her hand, but knowing that she was my buddy made me feel like I was someone. It was a good learning experience, in that I realized that I could have female friends just as easily as having male friends. This was something that I carried throughout my growing up years. In fact, I always said that most of my female friends were my wife's best friends.

My high school years, from 1934 through 1938, were not extraordinary. I served as a "GO GETTER" and helped with the distribution of tickets for some of the school activities. I traveled with the basketball team for 3 years, and found that to be very invigorating and educational. Coach Moskowitz let me practice with the team, even though I didn't wear a uniform. I could even shoot baskets from the centerline, which was quite an accomplishment for a little fellow. Graduation day in June1938, found me on the front of the graduation procession. First in line was getting to be a habit. One of my neighbors was graduating from a Physical Ed school in Manhattan, and I got very interested in the idea of College and being a Gym teacher. I discussed this with my mother, and she agreed that it was a good idea. When I asked my father to agree, he said, in his usual apathy, "Go get a job". I had already learned from past experience that my mother made most of the decisions, and I let her be my advocate. We finally got my dad to agree, and I enrolled in the Savage School for Physical Education.

Savage School for Physical Education had a curriculum that was a three year training course for a diploma. Many of the gym teachers in the NYC Board of Ed had graduated from this school and were accepted into teaching, provided they took 4th year courses to get their Bachelors Degree. I believe that this was the only college in the country that could make those arrangements. Savage was the third best rated school for Physical Education training in the country. Iowa State teachers College was the 1st and Cortland State Teachers College in upstate New York was the 2nd. I was heading into a very highly rated college atmosphere, and I was ready for the challenge. I had visions of graduating and entering the teaching profession in the NYC public schools. I wanted to work with children, and hoped that someday I would own a summer camp. I was trained in almost every sport, and would be able to coach school sports if I ever got to be a teacher. I knew that many of the gym teachers in the NYC school system had graduated from Savage School, and began to teach while they were in College, earning their 4th year credits, which they needed for their BA degrees. I was hoping to follow in their footsteps.

I graduated from Savage School in June 1941, and, not surprisingly, I was the first one in the graduation procession down the aisle, for the third time. However, by this time, I didn't give a second thought to my height. I had a lot of good schooling under my belt, and I was ready to take on any challenge that confronted me. Now, I had some free time and was spending it with the fellows with whom I had grown up.

My closest buddy, Blackie, asked me if I wanted to buy a car, and be his partner. He had a chance to buy a 1937 Oldsmobile with a rumble seat for $100 dollars, and he needed some help with the payment, I agreed, and we bought the car. We decided to share the car on an every other day schedule, and put in a few gallons of gas every day that either of us used the car. That worked out pretty well, and sometimes we had dates together.

I don't remember the date. but I asked Blackie to use the car on one of his days because I had a date with one of our girls. Her name was Sherry, and I had made a date with her for that night. Blackie said it was impossible because he had a date with her also. We called Sherry, and told her of the conflict, and she admitted that she erred, and made dates with both of us. Let me just add that Sherry was a member of the group and not a steady date with any of us. There was no problem, and she said that Blackie asked her first, and that she would ask her neighbor to be my date for the evening. I agreed to this arrangement, and we were to pick the girls up at 7:30 that evening.

When we got to Sherry's house, she was out front talking to my date, whose name was Dorothy Goldstein. First impressions were very interesting because she was wearing a loose hanging house-dress, her hair was in pin curls, and her smile showed braces on her top front teeth. She was very friendly and relaxed and comfortable, but said that she wasn't interested in riding in the back rumble seat. She said that, if I didn't mind, she would rather just sit out front of the house and talk. I had no problem with that, and we spent a lovely time, just talking and becoming acquainted. We walked up and down the street for a while, and it was time to say good night. I walked her to her door, and asked her if I could call her again. She agreed, and I said good night. This was the summer of 1941. Dorothy and I had several dates, and we were getting very warm and friendly. We had been to Coney Island a few times, and I showed her the concession stands where I worked. She had met most of my friends, and had been to my home for dinner with the family. I had been to her home for dinner with her family, and I was being accepted as a good friend and a likeable companion for Dorothy. My mind was set on making this girl my future wife, but I didn't make any aggressive moves. She was friendly and warm, and even kissed me goodnight when I left her after an evening out.

Europe was at war, and the entire world was getting concerned. Our government had instituted a draft, and was calling up our men for service in the military. At that time, the draft was taking one member from each family, and my brother Simon was in the draft. I new that someday my turn would come, and I would be called.

As a Physical Education graduate, I was offered a commission in the Navy, to serve as a training officer at the Great Lakes Naval Training Center. Former Heavyweight Boxing champion Gene Tunney was Director, and was recruiting men to serve as trainers for the inductees in the Navy. I could receive a commission as an Ensign, and be assigned to duty out there. This was a tremendously inter-esting offer, and I brought it home to discuss with my mother. After much discussion, my mother recommended that I wait. There was no rush for me to join up. I guess she didn't want to see two of her sons going into the service at the same time. Her female intuition was taking charge again.

By that time, Simon was engaged and 1A in the draft, and he was scheduled for September or October induction. He wanted to get married, but the draft was putting a hold on his plans. There was lots of talk about the United States joining in with our Allies in Europe, and we would be in it with the rest of them. So, after talking with my mom, we agreed that I would replace Simon in the draft, and he could get married. The draft was still taking only one from a family at that time, and he would be deferred.

I volunteered to go in his place. When I went for my physical, I was almost denied, because my feet were a little flat. I had a low arch, and my medical examiner was questioning my ability to perform. I encouraged him to look away from my feet and to pass me on the physical. I wanted to go in my brother's place. He passed the physical, and I was accepted.

I told all my friends that I was going into the Service, and that evening I went over to the Goldstein's to tell them the same decision. Dorothy was understanding and wished me well, and when I said good night to her mother, I said, "I'm coming home to marry your daughter". When I called Dorothy to say goodbye, her mother asked her what kind of nut is that schoolboy.

CHAPTER VI

I was enlisted on October 17, 1941, and was sworn in as a recruit with the Army Air Force. I was sent to Camp Dix, in New Jersey for indoctrination. After a few days, we were moved to Camp Lee, in Virginia, where I was to begin Medical training. It seems that my college training had a lot of science courses, and the Medical Officers figured that I could be a medic. I was assigned to the 9th Medical Battalion, and we started three months of very intensive training; constant drilling and training classes kept us busy and very tired at the end of the day. We were going to be using our training so that we could be "MASH" type units with combat units in the field. I was to be a surgical technician, and was learning how to function around the operating table. We were ready for assignment, and were waiting for orders to be issued. We had completed a very intensive training course, and we were equipped. The science classes at Savage School proved to be very helpful, and I felt confident in my being able to function with all of the new training and education I had received in basic training.

Camp Lee was a very well organized Army facility. We had nine medical battalions in training, and all of us had the identical schedules. We worked hard and long hours every weekday and had relaxed evening and weekend schedules. For the most part, we went to Richmond for our social evenings. There were several USO centers, and we made friends with the local girls, who volunteered to be hostesses. We got in with a very nice group of girls who invited us to their homes to meet their parents and enjoy evenings with them. We knew that this was a temporary stop over, and for the most part, we just enjoyed having someplace to go and someone to be with. Southern hospitality was very pleasant, and we Yankees were treated very nicely. I went home to Brooklyn on a few of the weekends and dated Dorothy as often as she would be available. We were getting more and more compatible and comfortable being with each other. I was hoping that this was the girl that I would be coming home to after the war was over.

It was early in December, while we were at a party in Richmond, eight of us, gabbing and listening to music on the radio. Suddenly the music was cut off, and an announcement was made. The voice was very serious, and the words were, "Gentlemen of Camp Lee, return to your barracks immediately. YOUR COUNTRY IS AT WAR". There was dead silence, and then one of the parents said," OK men, we'll drive you back to camp". We piled into two cars and were driven back to camp.

There was so much excitement and activity that none of us knew what was happening. We got back to our barracks and finally settled down, waiting for announcements or any information as to what or when we would be moving. It was about four days later when we finally got our travel orders. The 9th Medical Battalion was being ordered to the Bangor Maine Air Force Base. We would be working with, and be surrounded by pilots, engineers, mechanics and a complete roster of logistical personnel who were making up the newly activated 5th Army Air Force under the command of General George Kenny. Most of the enlisted personnel were in the Army about three months, the same as I. Life was getting more exciting because we had a new direction, and we knew that we were prepared for anything that we were asked to do or anyplace that we were told to go. We knew that something was about to happen, and we were going to be moving, but we didn't know when or where we were going.

It was early in February when we got our orders to go overseas, with the entire 5th Air Force. I was an acting corporal and had some extra privileges. I couldn't get a pass to go home to say goodbye, but I knew that we had a few days before we shipped out. We were ordered to close up shop and pack our equipment. I figured, with all the excitement and activity, that I could sneak out of camp, and get to

Brooklyn for a goodbye visit. I felt that I wouldn't be noticed and decided to risk going AWOL for two days. I got the train schedule and made it to the Bangor Station, and rode down to Grand Central Station in New York. I got a cab at the station and walked in on my parents, unannounced.

This was a momentous visit because I had to make it short and quick and cover a few bases before I headed back to Maine. After dinner, I called Dorothy and told her that I had to see her for a few minutes because I had to rush back to camp. Dad gave me the car keys and I drove over to Dorothy's house, picked her up and sat in the car for about an hour. We talked and I told her that I would be leaving for overseas. I didn't know where I was going yet, but I would let her know as soon as I was able. It was a very emotional feeling for me, and Dorothy was very responsive. When we went back up to the apartment, and I said goodbye to her parents, my last words were, "I'm coming back to marry your daughter". This was the second time I said that, and when I kissed Dorothy goodbye, I told her that I meant what I had just said. I got home and made arrangements to catch the early train out of Grand Central Station, and get back to Maine and camp.

It was snowing when I got up in the morning, and by the time I got to the station there were about two inches on the ground. It wasn't a heavy snow, but it was steady and kept coming down for the whole trip. When I left the train at the Bangor Station and got to the bus stop, there was no one around except for a hire car. I asked the driver if he would take me to the Air Base. He agreed, and as we were leaving the curb, two Medical Officers approached the car and asked if they could ride back with me. This was a blessing in disguise because I had no pass and was trying to figure out an excuse for getting back into camp. I was very gracious, and welcomed them into the back seat. As we approached the gate, and the MP's noticed the passengers, they saluted and passed the car into camp. That was a big relief for me, and I knew that I was home free.

I got into the barracks without being noticed, and when I saw that my barracks bag was filled, and in line with all the others, I knew that my buddies had covered for me, and that everything would be alright. So, I forgot about being hungry, and sat on my empty cot, and waited, along with the others for orders to move. I was really a little Jewish boy from Brooklyn, who got very lucky. We got our moving orders around 2 PM, and headed for the troop trains that were to take us to Boston. We were told that we were going to the Middle East.

CHAPTER VII

We arrived in Boston, got off the train, and were loaded onto buses, and were taken to Boston Harbor to get on board ship. The date was February 17, 1942, and we were boarding the QUEEN MARY. We were eleven thousand troops, the US Army 5th Air Force and we were composed of pilots, engineers, co-pilots, staff officers, and about eight thousand enlisted men. We would be setting out for someplace in the Pacific to fight the Japanese. Rumor had it that we were going to reinforce the Air Force and ground troops in Java, but no one could confirm it.

My stateroom, along with eight other medical personnel, was on the Promenade deck, which separated the upper decks where the Officers were quartered away from the enlisted men. We set up a temporary medical office alongside the Purser's Office. Most of the enlisted men were still being checked medically, and we were setting up inoculation centers, to give preventative shots to all of the personnel on the ship. My bunk was the top of a triple tier which surrounded the stateroom. The only open space was the bathroom area. My bunk had an air vent blowing fresh air into the room, and it wasn't very comfortable. I found a solution and claimed the bathtub for my bunk. I outranked the other eight men, as I was an acting Sergeant, so my decision wasn't questioned. The problem was solved, and it was a routine for me every day. I put the mattress on the bed in the morning and took it down to the tub in the evening. Little did I know that this was going to be a long trip that would last forty days.

The first order of business was to start the inoculation program, and we set it up. We had the men pass down the line on both sides of the tables. Typhus, tetanus, and Yellow Fever shots were administered, shooting the serums into both arms at the same time. It was an assembly line effort that worked like clockwork, and it took five days to complete the shots with everyone, including the Officers, getting the three shots.

It was hard to imagine, but meals were quite an endeavor. There were three shifts for every meal, which started at 7AM every day. Breakfast for the entire personnel lasted until 10 AM. Lunch started at noon, and lasted until 3 PM. Dinner started at 6 PM and lasted until 9 PM. The evening activity was a movie, or if you could find playing cards, there were card games. This ship was really crowded, and there wasn't much free space to roam around in. Many of us spent as much free time as was available out on the open deck. We were heading south, and the weather was nice and balmy after the second day out. We were told that we were heading for Key West for refueling and refitting our food supplies. We had a lot of mouths to feed, and the kitchen was working twelve hours a day. The only gripe was that this was a British ship, with a British crew. The food was a little strange, with kidneys or medium well done bacon, with powdered eggs. It was not the most palatable of food. However, we managed to eat, and no one went hungry.

On the third day out, we had a medical problem when we found one of the enlisted men in the cabin next to ours had the measles. We immediately quarantined that cabin and checked all of the men. Fortunately, there was only one patient. We got the approval from our Medical Officer, and were allowed to get meals for this cabin from the Officer's Mess. I must admit that my bunkmates and I benefited from this arrangement because the kitchen help filled all of my requests for meals for the sick people. My cabin mates would have voted for me to be a General if they could because they ate the same food as the quarantined guys ate, which was from the Officer's dining room. This only lasted for about a week, and then the cabin was removed from the quarantine. Now, we all had to go back to the routine of the rest of the ship.

When we got to Key West, that was the first time we saw any life, except for an occasional bird flying our way. We were told that the ship traveled at 17 knots per hour, and that nothing afloat could catch it.

That was fine, but we had no escort, and we could maybe run into something. We made a quick stop at Trinidad to pick up mail and some other materiel and then headed south to Rio De Janiero.

Entering the harbor in the early morning was really a thrilling sight. The first thing we saw was the statue of Christ on the mountaintop, and even for a non-believer, it was an awesome sight. As we got deeper into the harbor, sail boats started to come out to greet us. When we dropped anchor, the sail boats cruised around the ship with bikini clad women waving bandannas and men waving their hats, it was a beautiful greeting. The rails were jammed with GI's who were waving back. Some of the younger men were diving for the coins and trinkets that some of the men were throwing down to them. I can still visualize this activity.

We were refueled and refitted with food and necessities, and we were ready to move out, when we were told that we were heading for Capetown, South Africa. This was a Southeastern direction, across the South Atlantic Ocean, across lots of open water. We had no escort, and we were getting deeper and deeper into strange waters. I think that we had volunteer lookouts by the hundreds for this part of the trip. We were sitting ducks if we ran into the enemy. We didn't have any armament on the Queen Mary. We were Air Force personnel, and none of us were trained for ground combat conditions.

The ship arrived in Capetown, South Africa in the early morning, and it was a very welcomed sight. We dropped anchor and started loading provisions and fuel for another leg of our journey. We lay at anchor for a few days with nothing to do. We were not moving, and we had no idea of what was to happen next. Some of the men made fishing lines and dropped them over the side to catch fish. No luck, because there were plenty of sharks swimming around the ship. Part of the provisions included a new drink called Ginger Beer, which was a non-alcoholic drink. It didn't go over too well because very few of us Yanks drank it. The British crew loved the drink, why I don't know, because it had no sweet taste.

We finally pulled anchor and left the harbor, heading northeast, which was what we expected. We were told that we were heading for Java. When we looked at a map of the potential areas, we realized that this was taking us up into the areas where the Japanese were very active. They were in the Philippines and the surrounding areas, and were bombing the Northern Territory of Australia. This was our destination, but we didn't know where the ship was going to pull in. We were now heading north.

After three days, we stopped in the middle of the Ocean and were dead in the water. Rumors started again, and then an announcement came over the loud speaker. Java had fallen to the Japanese, and our airmen and soldiers were captured and were prisoners. We received orders to change direction, and head south towards Australia. There was a lot of uncertainty and confusion, and a lot of anxiety. We were greenies, not very experienced, and very confused. The only pleasant thought was that we were heading to a land that spoke our kind of language, and we would finally get our feet on solid ground again. There was a lot of uncertainty in not knowing what was happening up north, where all the fighting was going on.

CHAPTER VIII

We sailed through the Bluffs of Sydney Harbor, two arms, reaching out into the ocean, welcoming us in. We had no idea as to what we were heading into, or how we would be received, but we were heading into friendly territory, and we knew that we were expected, and we would be welcome. The Queen Mary was a big ship, and this was a Big Harbor. But we didn't see any docking areas, and we wondered where we would dock. There were many little ferries in the harbor, and a bridge from the mainland to one of the arms. The Aussies call it the Harbor Bridge, but we renamed it the "coathanger". It is a very pretty bridge, and fits perfectly into the landscape of the beautiful entrance to the city of Sydney, Australia.

It didn't take too long, and ferries started coming out in a steady flow. Troops were debarked, and the landing of the Americans on friendly soil was taking place. It was early evening when we were shuttled up to the Randwick Racecourse where we were to be billeted. Stables were redone and made into barracks, and the entire facility was turned over to us for our home base. We were transported on trolleys, from the Circular Quay through town, out to the racetrack. The civilians were cheering and waving to us and handed us copies of the local paper. The headlines said." General Blamey to establish Brisbane defense perimeter". The plan was to allow the Japanese to advance down from Darwin, and the Australian Home Guard would defend Brisbane.

When I think back, conjecturing about Generals Blamey's plan, if that had happened, the Japanese would be in Australia today. That was the news headline the day we came ashore in Sydney.

The entire U.S. Army 5th Air Force, had arrived in Australia after forty days at sea. We were a complete unit, but not functioning because we had NO PLANES. We were in limbo until something positive could be accomplished, and we were made whole again. The date was March 1942, and the Australian men of fighting age were in combat in the Middle East, fighting the Germans for the past three years.

Australia is where the song "They're either too young or too old" was written. Just imagine, all of these wonderful people dancing in the streets, welcoming their saviors. We really felt great, and realized that this was going to be a wonderful place to be stationed. It certainly started out that way.

After settling into the new camp, we got organized, and as one of the few NCO's, I got the first crack at time off the base. Arriving in Sydney coincided with the Jewish Holiday, Passover, and I headed out in search of a Synagogue. I found the Central Synagogue and was greeted with open arms. I was the first American soldier to be there, and was greeted by a lovely gentleman named Leo Rose. He invited me home for dinner and to meet his wife and daughter Janice. The evening was perfect, the food was great, and I felt perfectly at ease in a foreign land. This was the beginning of a friendship that has continued all these years. Jan and I have been visiting each other and watching the families grow up for the past sixty four years. This is a very important and meaningful relationship, and our families remain very close.

We settled in and started moving around, learning the ins and outs of this new environment. We got invitations, made new friends, and attended social events and were getting very comfortable in the racetrack barracks. We were accepted completely, and were becoming a part of the community.

Social life was very accessible, and we had many areas to visit. There were social clubs where there were refreshments and group activities. Austerity conditions were in effect, and there weren't many restaurants available. Food was not readily available as Australia is an Island Continent, and in wartime, there weren't too many ships on the ocean. Japanese submarines were often spotted, and since there were no ships coming or going submarines weren't seen as a problem. There were severe shortages throughout the Country, and the only food available was what was grown in the farm lands of the "Outback". The Australian Home Guard had captured a two passenger Japanese submarine just inside Sydney Harbor. It seems that the sub ran out of fuel and food, and just had to surface or starve. Somewhere in one of the Sydney coastal suburbs, that submarine is still on display.

There were many young women, who had been without companionship for three years and they were very glad to have male escorts again. We were in a different cultural environment, and we had to adapt to a new social attitude. We had to learn our P's and Q's all over again. It was working very nicely, and we were learning the local colloquialisms. Their speech had a little twang, almost American, but not British. It didn't take too long before we were using the speech mannerisms ourselves. It was very relaxing and congenial.

There was total austerity in Australia. Restaurants had limited food, prices were controlled, bars had limited alcohol, and the beer was warm. There were no drinks with ice in restaurants. There was a special sitting room for the ladies as they were not allowed to sit at the bar. The bars were opened in the afternoon from 2 to 4 PM. When it was time to close, the bartender called out, "Time Gentlemen", and that was the last time you could order a drink. The daily ration was one bottle of scotch, one bottle of rye and one bottle of gin. The beer tap was open until the call for the end of the drinking period. Lunch and dinner menus were price fixed, and you couldn't spend more than 8 Shillings for any meal. There was a serious shortage of food supply.

We remained in Sydney for about 6 weeks, and then we learned that the Air Transport Command would be flying B-17's from California, and our 5th Air Force would be supplied with enough aircraft to become operational. It was time to start packing and saying goodbye to the new friends that we had made. Pilots and crews were briefed, ground crews were organized, the medical department was getting all of our supplies itemized and packed. When we got the final order to begin moving out, we were ready and waiting.

CHAPTER IX

We boarded a troop ship in the harbor and headed north to Port Moresby, New Guinea where our air base was to be. Now we knew that this was the moment, and we were going to be involved in the action. As we sailed further north, we began to realize that we were nearing the equator, and it was hot up there. We were giving malaria shots, and a briefing about where we were going, and what to expect when we got there. Little did we know that we were disembarking in an area that was completely uninhabited, except for a few native village communities. We brought everything with us, including water tanks, and purifying chemicals. This was certainly going to be a "start from scratch" encampment. Our Commanding General was named Kenny, a short man, but a powerful personality. He had the respect of the entire personnel.

It was the middle of June 1942, and I was sitting on the deck of a troopship heading north from Brisbane, along with the rest of the personnel of the 5th Air Force. I was trying to compose a letter to a girl in Brisbane. She had been a very good friend and a very nice companion for the past 2 months. I was trying to think of words of apology, for having hurt her feelings, which ended our friendship. I never sent the letter, but I kept the copy.

We were finally going into what we assumed was the beginning of our actual time in the combat area. We were going north to establish an air base which was to be a part of the defense of Australia, and was to be the beginning of the Allied push to get the Japanese invaders to move back or be eliminated.

Our first briefing aboard ship was to tell us that we were the front line of the defending forces. Our base was to be set up on the southern end of the Kakoda Pass, which we learned was the separation point between us and the Japanese forces. There was an Australian Battalion of Engineers cutting an airfield out of the jungle. We were going to be camped at that airfield, and we would have to set up our medical unit in the adjoining areas. We were the first "MASH" unit in the South Pacific. We later learned that we were in New Guinea before General McArthur left the Philippines.

I guess we were too new at the military business to be scared of what we were getting into. When we were dropped at our camp site, we were instructed to find a suitable spot to bed down and were told to dig a slit trench to sleep in. We learned that the Japanese Zero aircraft were constantly dropping bombs on the area, and the shrapnel could inflict serious wounds. We were medics and ground crews and weren't equipped for that kind of work, so we had to make do. We used our knives and forks from our mess kits to dig. It wasn't difficult because this was a pretty sandy area, and we didn't have to worry about rocks and boulders. Needless to say, it was very time consuming, and we were finished digging in time to get to bed. It was dark, we ate our packaged food, and we were really tired enough to sleep standing up if we had to.

Our Chaplain was in the trench next to mine, and we had a warning of an aircraft attack coming in. We dropped into the trenches and started sweating. The Chaplain was cheering us up, and mentioned that he wished he had his sacramental wine in there with him. I asked him where it was, and told him I would get it for him. I crawled out, found his knapsack, and brought it back to him. When I crawled back into my little trench, I realized that I was stupid for exposing myself to danger. It was a lesson in awareness, and I didn't make that kind of foolish action again. I was learning to be alert and more careful every day.

The daily bombings, usually around mealtimes, were a constant reminder of the dangers in the area, and we were always on the alert. Passwords were assigned to us, and were to be used whenever any of us moved around after dark. We were told that the Japanese had difficulty pronouncing their "L", and our passwords were

WOOLWORTH, WOOLLOMALOO, or WALLUMBA, which were changed every day. Our security was ordered to challenge any moving person, and if he didn't respond properly, we were to shoot and ask questions later.

It didn't take too many days before we had a kitchen and mess tent set up. The activities and schedules were getting to be pretty routine. Supplies were coming in from Port Moresby, and our camp was beginning to look like a little community of tents. Our base was called the 17 Mile Airdrome, and the Australian Engineers were attached to our camp. The Engineers had portable baking equipment, and we contributed flour and stuff, so that we had fresh baked bread every day. The only glitch was that it was an open air bake oven, and whatever was flying got mixed into the dough. For the first few days, we picked the little dark spots out of the bread, and then realized that all we had left was the crust. The Aussies were eating the whole thing, as is, and none of them were getting sick. Then we realized that we had to change our ways. We had margarine for a spread, and covered the bread so we didn't see the spots. That worked for a while, and then we realized that the slices didn't have to be covered, we could eat it as the Aussies did.

We were getting used to these daily visits by the Japanese planes, and only had the Australian Whirlaway, two seater biplanes to defend us, so it was a daily routine of jumping in and out of the trenches whenever the raids were on. These Australian fighter planes had front mounted machine guns. There was an occasion when the Whiraways were up, trying to chase the zeros when one of our planes was shot down. The Australian pilot had bailed out and was floating down. As he was coming down, one of the zeros circled and shot through his parachute. The pilot plummeted to the ground, and was killed. Several days later, we shot down a zero and captured the injured pilot. He was brought into our infirmary, and we had him examined. He had fractured arms and legs and was badly injured. We had orders to try to fix him up so that he could be interrogated by our G2 personnel.

We tried to keep him alive with medications, but the pain killers didn't work, and he succumbed to his injuries. We went back to our normal routine, which included ambulance duty every day and night at the airfield tower. We were finally getting B17's, which were being flown over by the Air Transport Command pilots. Our pilots were finally getting their own planes, and we would be going on the offensive. The time was coming for payback. We were the front line airfield and became very active during the next few weeks.

This was the period when the American Navy was engaging the Japanese Navy in the Coral and Bismarck Sea battles. Our base was being used for refueling our bombers, caring for the wounded airmen, and sending the planes out again. It was a very hectic time, and the hours were not counted. There were constant day and night flights, all of which were successful. The Japanese fleets in the Coral Sea and Bismarck Sea were defeated. Most of the Japanese fleet was sunk, and the rest just scattered and fled North.

We had some aircraft losses, but they were at a minimum. This action was the first successful counter attack by our forces in this area. The 5th Air Force received a Presidential Citation commendation for each of these battles, and we on the ground shared in these honors. We were presented with the Presidential Citation device, which included a gold star.

We were beginning to feel as though we were turning the battles in our favor, and the general feeling in the outfit was very happy. One night the siren alert went off, and we all jumped into our trenches, which we had finally dug deep enough and long enough to hold four men. We were being bombed by light aircraft, and one of the 500 pound bombs landed about 50 feet from the trench that I was in. The concussion was so intense that it blew my helmet off. The sound of the blast was tremendous and shook us up, spattering us with debris from the explosion. Fortunately, no one was injured, but we were as scared as could be. Several nights later, while I was on ambulance duty with Dr. Goldman at the tower on the airfield, I decided to stretch out on the gurney in the rear of the ambulance. Dr. Goldman remained in the passenger seat up front. The siren on top of the tower went off. An invading Japanese plane had come in and was dropping little daisy cutter bombs on the center of the airstrip. I was awakened by all the excitement and found that Dr. Goldman was hit with shrapnel in his lower legs. I had slept through the entire alarm alert, and wasn't aware of any activity until I heard the shouting and noise of the bombs.

I helped pull the doctor out of the ambulance and started working on containing the loss of blood. We put tourniquets on his thighs, bandaged and disinfected the wounds and wrapped him for removal to a safe area. He was transported to the infirmary and flown out to Townsville, in Australia, the next morning. We later learned that he was recovering and was to be flown to Sydney for further treatment. This was my second encounter with personal involvement in this war.

There was another air raid incident that was memorable and worth writing about. We were jumping into our trenches when the alarm went off, and one of my tent mates jumped in and landed on the outside of his left foot. He was a very tall and heavy fellow, and the impact threw his ankle out of position, forcing one of his leg bones to break through the skin. We pulled the twisted foot back into position and managed to reset the bone into its normal area. After filling the open wound with Sulfanilamide powder, we wrapped and tied the wound securely. We got him into an ambulance, and he was on his way to the emergency field hospital. A few weeks later, we learned that this emergency help had saved his foot. He had recovered and was able to use his foot again. I guess that the surgical procedures repaired all of the damage from the fall.

This was summertime, and hot and humid, and we were getting acclimated to the conditions. We even had a good relationship with the local aboriginals, who were paid to do some of our manual labors. They helped build us a few thatched buildings for our mess halls and a thatch hut for our emergency infirmary. Their women came through camp with trays of native fruits and vegetables, which we bought from them. There was a strict taboo in regards to the women. They were uneducated to our ways, and most of them wore wrap around skirts, and were bare breasted. This was natural for them, because their men just wore a loincloth and were bare chested. We wore as little as possible because of the heat, and many times, when off duty, we lay on our bunks in under shorts and nothing else. When the women passed through the tents, selling their fruits, it was normal. Sometimes, one of the guys would pass a remark like, "you know, they're getting to look more and more interesting every day". Fortunately, we had no incidents.

We didn't ask the aboriginals to get the coconuts down from the trees for us because we needed quite a few. Besides, they could climb the trees themselves, and get what they wanted, very easily. Our security personnel were asked to shoot down some birds for the aboriginals, so they could eat them for their food. That was a quid pro quo action, as the aboriginals were very friendly and helpful.

The nights were very boring, and mostly we just shot the breeze, wrote letters, or went to sleep early. One night, while we were just passing time, I got the idea of making a concoction of drink using some of our alcohol. We had 180 proof alcohol for sterilization purposes,, and I remembered some of my father's early days activities, when he was a bootlegger. I decided to make our own "Bombo" juice. I borrowed Signal Corps pole climbers and a long rope. I shimmied myself up a coconut tree with the rope and lowered the rope. One of the men tied a machine gun to the rope and I pulled it up. Then, I balanced myself and aimed the gun at the tree, just below the growth of coconuts, and shot through the trunk of the tree. Down came the whole top, coconuts and all. Now we had the ingredients to mix with the alcohol.

We found an empty five gallon can, added two gallons of 180 proof alcohol, two gallons of water, one gallon of coconut juice, dried raisins, apricots, and a vent seal for the cap, and the mix was complete. We dug a hole and buried the can so that it could be cooler than the surface air. Two weeks of fermentation was all we asked for, and we had a finished product. We left it to age for two weeks, and then dug it up. We decided to sample the concoction after the evening dinner and gathered in the Infirmary. Each of us had his mess cup, and we poured a little into each cup. To be very honest, this drink had a pleasant taste, considering the additives, but it was powerful. I don't think that we could do anything but sip it a little at a time. It had a kick to it and could be intoxicating.

It was a successful venture, and we even took the two nurses into our confidence. They were very friendly Officers and were regular guys. They kept our secret, and we managed to keep this escapade to ourselves. When it came time to make another batch, we included the Doctors, and they didn't object either.

It was a few weeks after the air raid where Captain Goldman was shot up, that I was called into the CO's office, and told that I would have to leave the unit. It was determined that I had lost a lot of my hearing, and I would be in jeopardy if I remained. I was offered the opportunity to be sent home for medical discharge. This was mid summer 1942.

Our unit had received Two Presidential Citations. We were advancing on the Japanese and were regaining lost areas and islands. We were the first in action, and even got here before General McArthur left the Philippines and walked ashore at Hollandia. I requested to be reassigned back to Australia and put on limited duty service. I still had the idea that I was going back home to become a Gym teacher. My wish was granted, and I returned to Brisbane as a sergeant, and was assigned to the Far East Command, Rear Echelon Headquarters detachment in Brisbane, Queensland, at an airfield called Mascot Field, which was in the outskirts of Brisbane.

CHAPTER X

I was assigned to the Medical Detachment of the replacement depot. I soon learned that the base was the jumping off location for all troops coming to the South Pacific. All incoming troops had to be checked out medically, and oriented into units for which they were trained. Our job was to see that the new troops were properly outfitted to go into combat and that they were physically ready. I was assigned to the Dental section, and was taught how to do dental examinations. Our Dental Chief was anxious to see that all of the men had healthy teeth before they went into the combat areas. My chief, Dr Malcolm Galvin, was a stickler, and he believed in preventative dentistry. He was so determined that he checked my mouth and told me that I didn't need my wisdom teeth. When it was a quiet time, he got me into the chair, and treated me to his expertise. He removed my four wisdom teeth, in two visits, using a lever technique. He extracted two teeth at a time, both on one side of my mouth, and I didn't have too much inconvenience. I healed very quickly, and never knew any difference. He was right in that I didn't need the wisdom teeth to chew properly.

There was a group of new recruits that were being indoctrinated. One of the men had severely extended "buck" teeth, and Dr Galvin arranged to do some serious work on this GI. Dr Galvin pulled the teeth, arranged to have permanent replacements fitted, and kept the soldier behind until he was fitted with the new permanent teeth. He looked like a new man, and couldn't thank him enough for what he did.

I was getting very adept at the examinations, and was doing scaling and gum treatments in preparation for dental work that had to be done. I wore a white coat, as did the Dentists, and some of the guys even called me "doc". I really enjoyed the work, and there was a time when I had a Colonel in the chair. When I very casually said. "spit please, Colonel", he had to listen to me, and he spit.

There was a new group of replacements who were passing through, and I recognized a cousin on my fathers' side as one of the new recruits. I checked his teeth and recommended that he be held back for further work. I managed to keep him in Brisbane for 3 weeks before he had to be released and sent up to his unit.

Dr. Galvin was a man from Kansas with a pleasant disposition. He smoked cigarettes, using a cigarette holder dangling from the side of his mouth. We had developed a very close relationship, and I could talk freely with him. One day, while we both were side by side in the latrine, I was mentioning about the dating I was involved with. He came back with a quick retort. He said," all you guys think about is your next date and what's going to happen. I just wish that I could pee without any discomfort". I was assigned as the assistant to Dr. Galvin for about six months and then was asked to take over a new assignment.

Our Colonel Jordan was opening a new department called, "Information and Education", and wanted someone to get it started. I was assigned to this work under the supervision of a Captain. We set up our Office and put up a large wall map, which showed the areas of combat and pointed out all of the advances that we were making up north. We became the focal point of the entire operation. When the USO troupes came over to entertain our troops, we assigned them to the areas where the troops were. One of the groups was Jack Benny, with Jerry Colonna and Frances Langford. They entertained us for one night, and then we had them fly out to the troops in the islands. He had many visitors fly in, and the Colonel arranged for us to have a Speed Graphic camera to take pictures of the greetings when the dignitaries got off the planes. I very quickly learned the techniques and became the unit photographer. It was my job to meet the incoming dignitaries when their planes landed. The Colonel would greet them as they deplaned, and I was snapping pictures of each individual as he shook hands with the Colonel.

Colonel Jordan was very pleased with this part of his responsibilities, and I erected a bulletin Board outside his Office. Most of the pictures taken with the VIP's were posted on the board. That must have made the Colonel a very happy camper. I even had several men assigned to work with us, and these privates were sent out to show films to General McArthur's family who were stationed in Brisbane. These guys eventually became Staff Sergeants.

I was in a very unique situation because I had no group responsibilities. When I was released from my dental assignment, I was placed on this Special Duty assignment. My job was to organize this new venture. We started a new group, and called it the Sunday Sports Entertainment Council and invited all of the Allied units to participate.

We had the US Army, Navy and Air Force. We included the Australian Army, Navy and Air Force, and the Dutch Air Force. We organized baseball games, with all of the units participating. Our Navy had some pro players in them, including Dom DiMaggio, of the Boston Red Sox, Phil Rizzuto, of the NY Yankees, Don Padgett, of the St Louis Browns, and Charlie Wagner of the Detroit Tigers. They were assigned to different Naval units, and were very competitive. Each of them was on a different baseball team. We used a local stadium for the games, and the attendance was very good in that the games were very interesting. We even tried our hands at cricket against the Australians, but that wasn't a good idea. Our players couldn't master the swinging techniques involved.

An interesting part of this activity was the fact that the man who was our Umpire was an American citizen. Mack Gillie came to Australia in 1935 and stayed. He married and started a family. He became a very good friend and hosted the American ballplayers at his home on many occasions. When I went to these parties, I always brought some food from our Commissary. That made it very easy for his wife, Mae, to be a very gracious hostess. Many evenings at the Gillie home saw Phil Rizzuto, Dom DiMaggio, Charlie Wagner and Don Padgett among the party guests.

I was in a very unique position, since I had no required check in schedule. I signed in monthly for my payroll and liquor and cigarette allotments. My only obligation was to keep my immediate Officer superiors aware of my activities and location. If I wanted to go into town, I could arrange for our chauffeur driven staff car for the ride. I even had Officer OD's as a uniform, but just put the stripes on the shirts. My Commanding Colonel Jordan became a friend, because I was constantly taking pictures of him meeting and greeting the dignitaries as the got off their planes. If there ever was a fat cat type of job, I had it, and I wasn't going to jeopardize this status. I learned how to grease the skids early on, and I played all my cards right.

I must admit that I had some bad days also. The story goes as follows. One night, in the PX, a few of us were having a few rum and cokes, and as usual, the stories were about our dates. I was in the middle of a story, and talking with an Australian twang, when I was interrupted by one of the 90 day wonders. He was part of a detachment of newly arrived 2nd Lieutenants who were assigned to our unit, and he addressed me with a very ethnic remark. I reacted with a swing at him with a coke bottle in my hand, and hit him on the side of the head. He fell backwards and was stunned. There was a little excitement, and I was ordered to go back to my barracks and stay there. I went to my quarters, and about an hour later, I was told that I was to remain restricted to quarters until further notice. The next afternoon, I was called into the Colonel's office to explain the incident. The Colonel heard my story and recommended that I apologize to the Lieutenant for hitting him, and he would forget the incident. I told the Colonel that I wouldn't apologize to him, but I would salute his uniform if it was hung on the flagpole, but not if the Lieutenant was in it. I wasn't going to apologize for an ethnic slur thrown at me. The Colonel had been a good friend, and he knew that I wasn't telling a fairy tale. He ordered me back to the barracks and I was still under restrictions.

The weekend was coming up, and I knew that I was restricted, so I did a lot of letter writing and reading. I got a message on Monday morning telling me that the Colonel wanted me to report to him in his Office. On the way to the office, I passed the bulletin Board. On first glance, I took a good look and saw the latest posting. I was astounded when I read the contents. In military lingo, it was simple. I quote, "Lieutenant R J Casey is hereby transferred, in grade, to another assignment, at Rockhampton, Queensland Air Base". When I got into the Colonel's Office, I didn't have a chance to say a word. The first words I heard were, "If I didn't know you to be truthful, you could have been in a lot of trouble. Now, go back to work and behave yourself". My friends were delighted, and everything went back to normal.

As I was one of the organizers of the Sunday Sports Committee I did the announcements and I was the commentator from the press box at the baseball park. It wasn't unusual for us to have the local dignitaries as invited guests. This was good public relations, and the Australians really enjoyed the events. I met a very lovely girl who was the daughter of one of the dignitaries in Brisbane. She attended one of our Sunday games with her father, and we became friends. In fact, we became good friends, and she was my date on most of the evenings that I was out of camp.

There was a night when some of us decided to go to a "country dance" in one of the suburbs. We went stag and were having a great time, dancing and making time with the local girls. I was whooping it up with my dancing partner, when I saw my "girlfriend", and she saw me. This was a disaster, and when I approached her to explain, she wouldn't listen, and turned away. Her last words were, "don't call me again". I didn't, and that ended a very good friendship. She was a good friend, and I felt very bad; but we were only friends, and no serious damage was done. I really couldn't blame her because there were no Australian young men around, as they all were up north in the Middle East fighting. She thought that I was her steady date, and I disappointed her. I never followed up or attempted to make contact again. I closed the book on a very nice part of my time in Brisbane.

The reports of victories up North were very encouraging, and our red pin markers were constantly moving on the map. The Japanese were being pushed back on all fronts, and there was a lot of elation and good cheer. General McArthur's tactics were magnificent. He was island hopping and leaving some of the Japanese troops stranded. Our troops didn't have to flush them out because they couldn't go anyplace. They were trapped, alone, and had to fend for themselves. This proved to be a very smart tactic, as there were no American casualties. If the Japanese didn't surrender, they would have to stay and rot on the islands.

The Philippines were reclaimed, and the headquarters was moving further north as the days progressed. Some of the Australian troops were returning home and were very welcome. The folks in Australia were beginning to think about the end of hostilities and were very happy. There was serious talk about our Command being dismantled, and we would be ordered to Manila because that was where the "Big Brass" was assembled.

We were alerted to prepare for transfer, and we packed our gear and footlockers for the move to the Philippines. I had a footlocker, filled with Tasmanian Cascade beer, which was a treasure, and it was going north with me. I sent the footlocker to the pier with the rest of the equipment. I was expecting to travel with the rest of the troops and get on the boat with all of the equipment. It wasn't meant to be because I got orders to stay behind to close up the Office. I would be leaving a few days later, and fly to Manila with some of the fighter pilots, who were going to join us. All I had with me was the barracks bag and some final reports, which had to be delivered to the CO at the new base.

CHAPTER XI

We flew out two days after the troop ship left the harbor. Our itinerary was to fly to a small island called Morotai for refueling, and then on to Biak, which was another small island, for a second refueling, before flying on to Manila. We left Brisbane on a C 47, which was piloted by Air Transport Command pilots.

We were 24 pilots, 6 enlisted men, sitting in bucket seats, with the luggage piled in the rear of the plane. We were flying over the ocean when suddenly we spotted an oil slick on the windows on the right side of the plane. The right engine was feathering and the propeller stopped spinning. Just picture the 24 pilots, who had completed many fighter missions, sitting helpless in the plane, as the ATC pilot was in command. He came back to calm us and said that the plane could fly on one engine. We were all dead quiet, and we were losing altitude slowly. The pilot came back and reassured us that we could make it to Morotai, but as a safeguard, we should be prepared to jettison the luggage if need be. The Gods were on our side because we just made a landing at the runway as we were losing altitude. We just barely ran the runway before the engine quit. We were out of fuel. We were told that the right engine would be replaced so that we could fly out the next afternoon. I could just imagine what was running through the combat pilots' minds. They had completed fifty missions and were heading home, and weren't in control of their plights. A young 2nd lieutenant pilot was in control of their destiny. But this was a very eventful evening because the radio announced the Japanese surrender. When we flew out on our way to Manila, the WAR WAS OVER. The Japanese had surrendered.

We landed in Manila, and we were transported to a tent camp, which was set up for the American troops. The war was over, and everyone was in high spirits. Now, we were waiting for orders to be transported back to the States. In the meantime, we had regular leave into Manila for recreation and other activities. I was one of the more privileged Americans and was invited to the local social functions. The Philippine families were very formal, and when they entertained, the adult members acted as chaperones. At the larger gatherings, there was food and music for entertainment. If we wanted to dance, we had to get permission from a parent, as the attitude was very formal. We learned to do what was necessary, and we were welcomed participants at these functions. We were living in a different social world and quickly learned the proper actions. We were treated with kindness, and the locals were very grateful to be free and able to function as they did before the war started.

For the most part, we were just marking time, awaiting orders. The few weeks that we were in Manila gave us time to reflect on the past three plus years that we were in the South Pacific. Those of us who were going home in one piece were thankful that it was finally over and that we could get back home to begin our lives all over again. I guess we all had matured enough to realize that it was a commitment that was completed and a job well done.

Our travel orders had arrived, and we were scheduled and assigned to several General Ships, which were to take us back to the States. Our destination was from Manila to Seattle, Washington. That was a real heartwarming announcement, and we were all packing for the journey home. Almost four years transpired since I enlisted in October of 1941. Now it was September of 1945, and I was going home. I was all in one piece, slightly damaged by my hearing loss but, nevertheless, safe, sane, and satisfied that I had been a good soldier, and proud of what I had been a part of. I was ready to go home, to family and a "girl I had left behind".

It was on this troopship, sitting on the deck as we sailed across the North Pacific, back to the States, that I started to reminisce and look back at the time I spent in Australia. I needed to think about the letter that I should have written before I left Brisbane to go into combat.

My time in Brisbane wasn't always work and planning. Let me reflect a bit. I had a very interesting social life and was dating the daughter of the Lord Mayor of Brisbane. Our dates were very friendly, and we got around to see and do a lot of interesting things. We have to remember that the Australian men were away from 1939, and we arrived in Australia in 1942. The women didn't have any eligible males around for more than 3 years. They had very few choices for companionship, and when we arrived, we became very desirable company. I was fortunate, through my contacts with the local political people, to meet this lovely girl. We became fast friends, and had an understanding that this friendship was not going to be a permanent commitment. We were going to be "kissing cousins", and it was a perfect arrangement.

On the boat trip from Brisbane to New Guinea, I started to write a letter of apology to the girl I had hurt in Brisbane. I thought it was the least I could do, as a reason to put some closure to what was the memory of a beautiful friendship. I had plenty of time on the trip. There was no reason to rush or be hasty with my words. It took about a week to complete. I realized that what I had put on paper was emotional and rhythmic, and had the beginning of what could be a poem. In short, I was going to keep this letter as an unfinished piece of writing. I never sent the apology. It wasn't until years later, when I was a married man, with a child and a piano in our apartment, that I looked at this composition and decided to put it to music. During my years in Australia, if I found a piano anywhere, I would sit down and play tunes that I remembered. I had the basic training in my learning years, and I had a solid foundation. I could still read notes and remembered the chording. Good teaching is never forgotten. I could never be a pianist, but I was a pretty good piano player. Anyway, this song that I was trying to compose had a title before it had music. I titled it ONE CARELESS MOMENT.

CHAPTER XII

It was a slow cruise back to Seattle, and, for the most part, we were all relaxed and counting the days till we got back to the States. Some of us set up poker games. Others just relaxed and counted the days. When we pulled into the harbor at Seattle, it was the happiest day in my life. We had been away almost four years, and when we disembarked, we were greeted as conquering heroes. It certainly was a wonderful feeling. My first thoughts were to find a telephone, and when I did, I called mom and dad to tell them that I was back in the States. The second call was to Dorothy, and I was very pleased to hear that she was very glad to hear from me, and was happy that I was home. I couldn't have gotten better news.

The next few days at the assembly compound were highly organized, and we were being grouped into sections, which were to be moved by trains, to different parts of the country. It took about a week to get all of us on our way, and finally, I was on the train, heading for New York City and home.

Needless to say, there was pandemonium in the Peskoff household when I got back home and into the family apartment. It had been four years since I left. All of the family who lived in Brooklyn, gathered in the apartment to greet me. I was the first one home. Simon and Herbie got home a few weeks after I returned. All three sons home in one piece. We were united again. It was a wonderful feeling, being home, with lots of memories to think about but grateful to have been able to get home safe. Some of my friends weren't as fortunate. They didn't make it back alive.

Now it was thinking time. What do I do? Do I go back to school to finish for my degree, or go to work for my Dad, who bought the business from his other two partners. I got some mail from my sister Shirley when I was overseas, telling me that Dad had bought the business for the boys to come back to. It wasn't my #1 choice, but I realized that I had to go to work. So, it was decided and mom said you work at Empire, and take school courses at night. That was the direction.

I enrolled at NYU for several heavy three point night courses and worked at Empire Boiler Company during the day. There wasn't much free time, but enough for me to begin to get social again. I called Dorothy as soon as I got unpacked, and made a date for the weekend. It was a real homecoming welcome at the Goldstein house when I drove over. I was greeted with open arms. Dorothy looked and acted exactly how I remembered. She was sweet and gentle and affectionate. No curlers in her hair and no braces on her teeth. I was one happy fellow, and was ready for a "full steam ahead" courtship.

I was running on all eight cylinders. Work was five days a week, school three nights a week, and Friday, Saturday, and Sunday dates were with Dorothy. Dinners at her house and my house were on a regular basis and were part of the routine. I was beginning to think that I wanted this to be a permanent part of my life. It was before Christmas 1945, about three months after I got home, that I asked Dorothy to marry me. I was really serious, and wanted to get my life settled and on the way to the future. Her father was recovering from his 2nd heart attack and was not in the best of health. It didn't take too long before she agreed, and with an engagement ring to seal the commitment, we set the date for March 30th.

Dorothy's uncle Sydney offered us the complete wedding at the Waldorf Hotel in the City. This was a great offer, but we declined. We agreed to have the ceremony in her brother Stanley's house because her father was too frail to subject him to a big time wedding with all the trimmings. This proved to be a very wise decision because he was able to attend, sitting on a chair under the "chupah", as he was too weak to stand for any length of time. And so we were married and lived in her bedroom in her parents' apartment.

We were married on March 30th, 1946. Ellen was born on February 28th, 1947. I remember rushing to the Hospital, after getting a call from the nurse. Dorothy was in labor and ready for delivery. Ellen was born, a little six pound girl, with black hair, while I was on the way to the hospital in Manhattan. I was driving in the snow all the way from Brooklyn to the hospital in midtown Manhattan, in a snowstorm. With no place to park, I left the car parked in front of a hydrant at the front of the hospital and raced upstairs.

I was hoping to find a boy so that I could name him William after his grandfather. This baby was the first in the family, and I wanted to have the first William. When I learned that my child was a girl, for the briefest moment, I was let down. But when I saw the child cuddled in her mother's arms, nothing else mattered. I had a lovely wife and a beautiful girl child. Watching her grow up was going to be a lifetime experience. Little did I know what the future would bring. I was a happy new first time father.

When I got down after the visit, I found a parking ticket on the windshield. The fine was 25 dollars. When I went to traffic court, I pleaded guilty with an explanation. The judge was very receptive and cancelled the violation. He then told me to put the $25 dollars into a bank account for the new baby. That was done and was the first savings account that I ever established.

While living in her apartment on E 2nd St. and working downtown on Flushing Avenue with no car, I had to depend on my brother Herb to pick me up and drop me off every day. About a month had passed, and one day Dorothy invited my brother Herb up to have breakfast with us before I went to work. He was very amazed to sit down for pancakes, and he told Dorothy that I never ate breakfast at home. That's all she had to hear. After that, it was juice and off to work. The only time I got breakfast at home was on the weekends.

It was about 6 months after the wedding I decided to give up the idea of earning the credits for my degree and quit classes. I couldn't get re-acclimated to schooling, and studying and lectures. My lack of normal hearing prevented me from properly taking notes or even following the dialogue in the lectures. I was not a happy camper in the classrooms.

We were still living in the apartment with Dorothy's parents, with a crib in our bedroom. Grandpa Sam Goldstein usually hovered over the crib with the bottle every time Ellen cried. And she was constantly crying. Ellen went from 6 to 7 pounds and stopped gaining weight. She was always hungry and constantly vomiting up her food as soon as she drank the bottle. When we called Doctor Dalven, and he came up to the apartment, he fed her the bottle and took her to his shoulder for the burp. She didn't burp. She just barfed up the milk. Then Dr. Dalven said we had a problem. He wanted us to see a Specialist. That was when we found out that her problem was called, "Pyloric Spasm". He explained his instructions and said that if this recommendation didn't solve the problem, Ellen would have to be operated on to correct the condition.

His prescription was a simple one. Dorothy was to make farina over a slow flame and stir it until it was very clumpy. When the concoction was thick enough that it wouldn't fall off the spatula, it was ready. It was to be separated into small ice cube portions and then fed to Ellen on a spatula and pushed into her mouth for her to swallow. This was supposed to force its way from the stomach through the pyloris valve and into the intestine. She was to be fed every 2 hours. We were to call him in 3 days for a report. Well, the miracle happened. The farina did the trick. She started to retain the food and, within a week, the food stayed down, the crying stopped, and life steadied. We could begin to set up a regular routine,, and Ellen slowly progressed. We could now live in a calm and organized fashion.

CHAPTER XIII

It was during the first few months, after Ellen was born, that I was left alone with her one day. I was in the living room reading, and when Dorothy came home from shopping, she saw me in the living room and wondered why I was not responding to the crying baby. I told her that I didn't hear her. It was at that time, fully aware of the consequences of my disability that I decided to go for help. I had been discharged with a zero disability because I wanted out fast and didn't want any delaying complications. So I took a trip to Manhattan and had a consultation with the American Legion representatives at the Veterans Administration

I filed a claim for disability at the V.A., and waited seven months for the processing. In the meantime, I arranged for visits and treatments at the Hearing Clinic of the V.A. and was part of a class of GI's undergoing hearing aid education. I learned to lip read, and graduated from this rehab class with a new hearing aid and brought it home for the first time. This was a new condition, something inserted in my ear, and I really was a little embarrassed. Getting adjusted was important. That night I went to a movie alone because I wanted to see what this new devise was capable of. Walking home after the movie in the dark, on a quiet street, I thought I was being followed. I started walking faster and faster, and noticed that the steps behind me were keeping up with me. As I approached my house, I started running up the steps and made it to the door. Out of breath, but safe inside, I suddenly realized that I was hearing my OWN footsteps.

I didn't know how much sound I was missing, and realized that I was going to be a lot more compatible in the world. The excuse that I heard what I had to, wasn't going to work in the future. Now

I could hear Ellen laugh and cry, and a new world of sound was back in my life.

I was one of the first GI's to go through the hearing rehabilitation program in NYC and was invited to speak at a mural dedication at the Hearing Clinic at the VA. I was to be one of the 3 speakers on the program. The chief of industrial medicine for NYS was one, Bernard Baruch was #2, and I was the third. I was never in such distinguished company, seeing has how Mr. Baruch had the ear of President Roosevelt and was one of his advisors. During the introductions he nudged me and asked me how come I was so comfortable with my hearing aid and he was having problems with static. He was wearing his hearing aid in his shirt pocket, and I guess he was hearing clothing rub. I had a harness with the aid inside a pouch, very much like wearing a bra. He reacted very quickly, and asked me where he could get such a harness. Not a problem, I said. Give me an address, and I will mail you one. I mailed a new harness to his address on Fifth Avenue. About a week later, I got a very nice thank you note. In retrospect, I wish I had saved it. Little did I know that he was a famous political person.

Several months later, I got a call from the Publicity Director for the Disabled American Veterans. I was asked if I would consider an interview, and tell my story about hearing rehabilitation. I agreed, and set up a time for the interview and the photo op. They were planning on using it in an issue of the Monthly DAV Journal. I was going to be a celebrity and have my story and picture in the magazine, which was to be published at the end of October of 1947.

I subsequently got a call from the DAV interviewer, apologizing to me profusely. He explained that their plans had to be changed and that I would understand. He was sending me an advance copy of the November Publication. The magazine arrived, and when I looked at the front cover, this was the headline. BERNARD BARUCH TOURS US ARMY HOSPITALS. I guess that I couldn't overrule that choice. He certainly was a better person to publicize this handicap condition. What was most important was the fact that I had turned the corner in my life and was coping with the outside world on a much more relaxed and comfortable level. My daily life was more interesting, and I was getting much more involved in the daily activities at home and in my community.

We stayed with Dorothy's parents for about a year, and I got edgy and wanted my own home. Finding an apartment was very difficult as lots of GI's were in the same position. One day, I read an advertisement offering a bunch of new homes in Manhattan Beach, Brooklyn. They were located at the end of the area, which was a real upscale neighborhood. The homes were little bungalow type houses, with a rear porch patio. It was small but very acceptable. The best part was that they were being offered to GIs for 66 hundred dollars with $600 dollars down payment, $60 dollars a month and carried a 30 year mortgage. I came home and asked my father for a loan of $600 so that I could tie up the house. And in his inimitable fashion, he said, "YOU DON'T NEED IT; go find an apartment".

We found our first apartment on Bedford Avenue in Brooklyn. This apartment was on the upper floor of a converted one family house. It was found through an agent who received an $800 dollar commission, and the rent was $90 dollars a month. It was ironic, because when I asked my father for the $600 dollar down payment for the house, he refused. But then he turned around and gave me the $800 dollars to pay the commission for the rental. I could never figure out his reasoning. But that was my father, and he was never going to change his ways.

My life had many little incidents that keep popping up as I write. This one was a really interesting occurrence. I was driving home from work on the Belt Parkway and was cut off by a very erratic driver. He cut across the front of my car and bumped the rear of the car in front of me. The car he bumped swerved and pulled up and stopped. The aggressive car driver swerved off the road, and stopped on the median island. He opened his door and fell out. We had all stopped our cars, and I pulled my car to the median and parked. When I got out, I saw that he was bleeding very badly from a cut on his neck. He had plenty to drink, and he was very incoherent. I pulled out a handkerchief and applied it to his neck to slow the bleeding. I used my own pressure to act as a tourniquet. One of the bystanders called 911, and it was about 7 minutes before the police and an ambulance got to the scene. It wasn't until the emergency medic took over that I was asked to release my pressure so that the bandaging could take place.

When I gave the Police Officer my name and phone number, it was a routine practice, and I had no problem giving out the information. The car that was rear ended was not damaged, except for a little dent in the bumper; the occupants of that car were not hurt. Everyone involved gave the Officer the required information, and we all went on our way. The ambulance took the injured person away, and traffic resumed normally.

About a week later, I got a call from an Attorney, and he asked me if I would be a witness to the accident. He was representing the car owner whose car was bumped. I told him that I wasn't interested because my time was worth money, and if he would pay me an hourly rate, I would make a statement. He wasn't very pleasant, and then I told him, that he could subpoena me, and I would tell the story, as I knew it. I also told him that his clients were hanging around the scene after the collision, and they didn't look hurt to me. I never got a second call from the Attorney.

Ellen was growing up, and we had bought a thoroughbred Scotch Terrier puppy for $400 dollars, whom we named McDuff of Bardene, after his grandfather "Bardene Bingo". Little did we know that his grandfather would win the Best of Show Ribbon at Madison Square Garden arena. Three months after we bought him, we got a call from his breeder, asking us if we would let her train him for show, and after he got his ribbon, we could set him up for stud. We could make lots of money breeding him to sell the pups. Dorothy and I decided that we wanted a pet and not a show dog. Poor "Duffy" was to live and die a virgin. But this pup was a magnificent pet. He learned quickly and strutted like a show dog. The entire neighborhood knew him and loved him as we did. He was welcome wherever we went and was a perfect guest. When we got invitations to visit, we were asked to bring Duffy along. He was always welcome as a member of our family.

CHAPTER **XIV**

When Ellen was about seven years old, we found our second apartment on East 29th Street in Brooklyn, and set up our own housekeeping in the upper apartment of a 2 family house. This apartment had an open porch outside the small bedroom, and we used it as a sun deck. Dorothy had a friend, Frances Hoodkiss, who lived two houses away, and had a son with cerebral palsy, and she was organizing a new chapter of women to help support a new fund raising effort for Cerebral Palsy victims. This was a very good activity, and Dorothy became the Secretary of this group. She became a very valuable member, and was productive for many years. This group raised over 25 thousand dollars for Cerebral Palsy. Frances Hoodkiss had 2 daughters, and the older one was the same age as Ellen, so that was a good compatible arrangement. Our two families were very interlocked, and many things were done together. We even spent time together vacationing in Florida, when we visited with Dorothy's parents who were in Florida for the winter.

Dorothy's father had a serious heart condition, and also suffered from pleurisy every winter. Sam and Sadie spent the winter months in Florida. This was their annual trip, and it helped avoid his pleurisy attacks. When Ellen was three years old, we decided to drive down to Florida and visit. It was our first long trip, and turned out to be a very enjoyable and pleasant trip. This was the first of many trips that we took, and Ellen proved to be a good traveler.

When Dorothy's parents returned to New York from Florida after one of their annual Florida trips, her mother had a stroke and went into a coma. It wasn't more than about two weeks in the hospital that Sadie passed away. We returned to our apartment after the funeral, and her father stayed with us for a few days. He decided that he wanted to go back to his apartment, and I drove him there on my way to work. Dorothy called me later in the day, and told me that her father couldn't be there alone and he wanted to come back to our home. He was packing some of his clothes, and when I picked him up after work, he was very happy to be rejoining us. He told me that he couldn't be alone. I had no objection because we had a very good relationship from the beginning, and I knew that he would not be a burden. He stayed with us and then started making plans to go south for his usual winter stay in Florida.

We had "Duffy" our little Scotch Terrier at the time, and the dog became a good companion for Dorothy's father. One night, after we were all asleep, the dog jumped up at us, and woke us with a whining cry. We got out of bed and followed him into the other bedroom. Dorothy's father was moaning and very uncomfortable. He needed some medication, and we got it for him. He became very comforted and relaxed, and went back to sleep. Duffy was a lifesaver, and he must have known that help was needed.

When he returned north after the winter season, he told us that he had met a very nice woman who became a very good friend. He told us that there was a time that he was under the weather and not getting out of the apartment. She knocked on his door and wanted to know how he was feeling. She saw that he was not well, and arranged to bring him cooked food and "Jewish Penicillin", which is chicken noodle soup. His recovery was much faster now. When he as able to get out on a regular basis, the two of them became a team. He wanted us to meet this lady who lived in New Jersey, and we made arrangements to go out and meet her family.

We took the trip, spent a very nice time with Eva's family, and realized that this was going to be a very happy future for the both of them. They were married shortly after that visit, and they returned to Florida and set up their own apartment. When we went south to visit them the next winter, we had lunch in their apartment. While we were eating, dad commented on how good a cook Eva was, and how well she prepared tuna salad. Eva knew that dad was from a kosher background, and she never questioned his eating requirements. When I asked her how she made the tuna salad, she confided in me, and said that it was really shrimp salad. He liked it, and ate it, and wouldn't know the difference, so there was no reason to tell him anything else.

They were married for about five years, and dad became ill and needed to be cared for in a nursing facility. We flew down and made arrangements, and we were there for two weeks, getting him settled in and comfortable. When we went north, we were sure that he would be getting the best of care, and would have Eva seeing him on a daily basis. His health was failing, and three months later he passed away quietly. We remained close with Eva until she passed away a few years later.

CHAPTER XV

After two years, we were offered a larger apartment in a 2 family home, across the street from the one we were living in. The apartment would give us more living space and had some amenities that were very important. It was street level and had a second entrance in the alley, at the side of the house. When I engaged the moving company, the truck was parked at the curb. All of the contents of the apartment were moved across the street on dollies. The piano was an easy move and rolled across very easily. There was a constant cross street movement for about three hours, and we were relocated.

We had access to the basement from our kitchen, which made it easier for me because, when I came home from work, I was tired and dirty, and had a need for a change of clothing. Many a day, I would strip my clothing in the hallway, and throw the dirty clothes down the steps into the basement. I would take a quick shower and dress for dinner, or go out, which was always a desirable alternative.

My work at Empire Boiler required me to go into basements to remove old heating equipment. This work was always a dirty job, and dust, asbestos, and soot were a part of my everyday work routine. I had the same routine five days a week. I would dress in work clothes in the morning, come home after work and leave my dirty clothes in the basement, and shower before dinner and the rest of the evening activity. I used to joke with my friends, when I told them that I changed my underwear twelve times a week. They would laugh until they found out what my routine was, and then they knew I wasn't kidding.

My new landlord, Max Michaels, was a friendly and agreeable person. I wanted to install 220 volt current for my air conditioner, and he approved the running of the new line from the basement. I made arrangements for the line to be connected to his apartment also so that he could benefit from the more powerful service. I told him that I would take complete responsibility for the care and maintenance of this apartment, and he would not have to worry about any repairs. That made him comfortable with our relationship, and our families became good friends as well as good neighbors. We redecorated the apartment, as Dorothy wanted, and we settled in comfortably in our new home.

We became active in the Synagogue as a family. Dad was saying "Kaddish" every evening, and I joined the Men's Club. Dorothy made friends with the women and joined the Sisterhood. I was invited to become a member of the Building Committee, as the Congregation was planning a new structure, and needed to raise funds. The existing building was a garage type structure, which had a tent attached to one side of the building. This tent was used to hold the High Holiday services because the building could not accommodate the Congregation for the Holiday Services.

The plans for the new building included a basement for the ballroom, the main floor for the Chapel and meeting room, which could be used as a ballroom, and the second floor, which was to be used for the Hebrew School, and would have class-rooms. The main Synagogue would be adjacent to the upper ballroom, and separated with a set of sliding panels, which could be closed off when necessary. This building would cost in excess of four hundred thousand dollars, and we were going to fundraise to make it happen.

The most interesting part of the design was that we were going to build the main structural foundations on half of the plan and use the tent as our meeting place. When the first half was completed, we abandoned the tent and moved the operating office and equipment into the finished half. It worked out as planned, and the building was started. We arranged for co-signers on the new mortgage and went to the bank for approval. The work began, and we were on our way to a new building to house Congregation Beth Shalom of Kings Bay.

When the construction was completed, and the building was refurbished, we made our plans for the rededication weekend. We agreed that the entire event was to be held on a Sunday, and the Community was to be invited to the rededication ceremony. We arranged for Governor Harriman to cut the ribbon and to be our guest speaker. The ceremonies started with a parade of cars through the neighborhood. We set up a portable "chupah", which led the procession, as the torah scrolls were carried under the canopy, by members of the Board of Directors. Our friends and neighbors were in the streets as we paraded through the streets and passed their houses. It was a memorable and beautifully planned parade.

When the parade finally got to the entrance of the Synagogue, the Community was told to enter the chapel and take their seats. When everyone was inside, the "chupah" was marched into the chapel, with the Torah Scrolls under the canopy. The procession continued down the center aisle, and when the Torah procession reached the Bimah, each of the scrolls was placed into the Ark by an Officer of the Congregation. The dedication program was now ready to begin. Congregation Beth Shalom was now whole again.

The dinner that evening was a black tie affair, which was a fundraiser, and the new ballroom was packed with a very happy Congregation. I was the toastmaster and had planned on a very dramatic opening statement. This was the first event on the first day of a newly dedicated building, and when I stood up to make the opening remarks, the lights in the ballroom were turned off. As I started to speak, the dimmers gradually came back on with my first words. I quoted from the Old Testament, and said "IN THE BEGINNING THERE WAS DARKNESS ON THE FACE OF THE EARTH, AND GOD SAID, LET THERE BE LIGHT. AND THERE WAS LIGHT". With the last word, the entire ballroom was flooded with all of the lights on full power.

There was a standing ovation for these opening remarks, and when everyone was back in their seats, the program began. The usual remarks from Officers and dignitaries were made, and the crowd was very pleased and happy. The dinner and dancing was a very pleasant anti-climax to a very successfully planned day, and, when it was over, everyone went home happy.

While I was working at Empire Boiler Company, I met one of our customers named David Chazen, who was a scrap iron dealer on the upper east side of Manhattan. It was our practice to deliver the scrap iron from our jobs in Manhattan, so that we wouldn't have to go back to Brooklyn with a loaded truck. He became a good friend and we discussed synagogue affiliations on many occasions. I learned that his daughter had become paralyzed after delivering a child, and he was a constant supplier of oxygen to her bedside. He learned that I was very active in my Synagogue, and as he was the President of his Synagogue, we had lots of common interests.

Years had passed and his congregation had diminished to the point that they had to sell to another Congregation in search of a spiritual home. New York State law requires that any money derived from a sale transaction must be redistributed to New York State Congregations. He offered me Twenty Thousand Dollars for my Congregation with a stipulation that I redonate ten thousand dollars to the Israel "Red Mogen Doved" ambulance organization in Jerusalem. There were no other stipulations. He didn't want name recognition in my Synagogue. It was a wonderful gesture, and after consulting with my Board of Directors, the donation and terms were accepted. Dave was a very charitable person, and he was anxious to be of help to me and to my Congregation. When Dave passed away, I went to his funeral and was amazed at the number of influential people who were there to eulogize him. He had been instrumental in raising funds for many of the Jewish Charities, and everyone wanted to remember this man for all of his wonderful endeavors.

This part of my life was very monumental, as it happened during the time I was serving as President of my Mens Club at Congregation Beth Shalom. I was attending a convention of members of the Mens Club leadership Officers of the Federation of Jewish Mens Clubs, which was held at the Concord Hotel in upstate New York. It was at the annual final dinner banquet, where the annual awards were being presented. I was sitting at one of the tables just below the head table. I looked up and saw Captain Goldman sitting in the honorees chair. When I stood up and waved, he appeared to recognize me, and he waved back.

When he got up to speak, he acknowledged my presence, and remarked that if it wasn't for me and my teammates in New Guinea, he would not have been here tonight to accept this honor. When I approached the dais after the speeches, he walked towards me and was using two canes to assist him in walking. I have to assume that his two legs were amputated below the knee. However, his life was saved, and he could continue being productive as a doctor. That day gave me a very happy outlook towards the future.

When my sister Shirley retired from her job at Maimonedes Hospital, she was tendered a retirement party. I attended the event with my brothers Simon and Herb, and we sat at the front center table. My sister Shirley worked as a representative of the Women's Division at the Hospital. Her responsibility was to see that the new mothers had the free samples, which were donated by many of the manufacturers. Simon and Herb were at the guest table in the front of the dining room with me. Ben Eisenstadt, the president of the hospital, was at the Dais, and was addressing the audience. He looked over at our able, and addressed us by introducing us as the men who made it possible for him to be the success that he was. It was my fathers $5000 dollars that started him on the road to the fortune that he had made with his SWEET AND LOW substitute for sugar product. When I would meet Ben Eisenstadt's son Marvin in the diner, he would say to me, "when are you going to stop coming for the "SWEET AND LOW". I would respond, and say, "stop complaining, Marvin, I could have been your partner."

CHAPTER XVI

Our Company, the Empire Used Boiler Supply Company, was a very important part of the New York City work force. We were the largest Supplier of used boiler parts in the City, and most of the contractors had to come to us for the repair parts that they needed for their job. Many of the homes in New York City were still being heated with coal, and most of the coal fired boiler manufacturers had gone out of business. We were picking up the coal furnaces that were being replaced with new oil fired furnaces. Our warehouse and storage yard were large enough to store and rehabilitate all of this old material and resell pieces as needed for the repair work.

When the contractors called for materials, if we didn't have what they wanted, they had to install new equipment. Our inventory was very large, and we realized that what was being discarded for new oil equipment had resale value. With our contacts with the new installers, we were able to arrange to remove the old equipment that they were replacing. Sometimes we paid for the materials, and most of the times, the contractors were glad to give us the old material if we would come and take it away. This put us in a very favorable position. We were a storage place for a great deal of repair parts, which were recycled and returned to use in many of the homes that needed the obsolete parts.

When I came out of the Army, and started working with my dad in his business, I found out that the Company had been using the Yellow Pages of the telephone directories, advertising the fact that "Empire" had repair parts for damaged heating plants. The Company was spending thousands of dollars a year in advertising in all of the sections of the Red Book. We were listed in every section of the book related to the industry. You could find the ads in Plumbing, Heating, Welding, Boiler Repair, and even the Scrap Iron section. The ads were 1/4 page ads and were very expensive.

I didn't know much about advertising, but I knew that we were very much in demand when the public had a heating problem. I realized that we couldn't solicit the public. We had to depend on the public finding us when they had a problem and needed help. With that in mind, I had a conference with the Telephone Company advertisement section people, and arranged to reduce the size of the ads, and highlight our name. This new approach to advertising was very successful, and we cut our costs by 2/3. Our motto was, "Have No Fear, Empire Is Here". It served us well, and we were very successful.

One of my neighbors at home was a Deputy Commissioner in the NYC Real Estate Department. He approached me one Saturday morning, in the Synagogue, and told me that there was a serious problem in his Department. He told me that the Mayor, John Lindsey, had put out an Executive Order, which stated that if there was any multiple dwelling in New York City without heat for more than 36 hours, the City would send a contractor in to make the repairs. The City would then bill the landlord for payment, and if it was not paid, the City would be empowered to put a lien on the property, and proceed to foreclosure. This was a magnificent new law, and very much needed, because there were a lot of slumlords n NYC, and they were not making the repairs in their buildings. There was only one big problem. New York City was in dire straits regarding their finance situation. There wasn't any money in the budget to pay for these repairs, and the contractors would not work without getting paid. His Office was in a dilemma, and he was asking for any help that I might offer him.

I talked it over with my brothers and Uncle Ed, and when I called Mr. Ekstein back, I told him that I could give him a proposition. I called my bank and asked for an open loan agreement, which would give me the money I needed to pay the contractors for working for me, as I would take the contracts, and sub the work out to them. When the loan agent was skeptical about financing an operation for a City that was almost bankrupt, I realized that I needed to change his thinking. I told him that there was a news report in which President Carter was involved, and the President said that there were many solutions for the problems in New York City, but bankruptcy wasn't one of them. He relented and gave us the line of credit that I was asking for.

I was to receive 1/3 profit for my labor, and 15% profit on my materials. This would allow me to hire the contractors and give them their rate, plus 1/2 of the profit on the materials. This was a win win situation because, if I didn't have any jobs, I didn't have any expenses. It was a perfect arrangement, and the wheels were rolling. I sat at my desk and took the job orders. I called the local contractors and assigned jobs to them, with the proviso that it didn't have to be the first job of the day. In the repair business, the first job is usually the one that pays for the labor for the crews. I knew that to be the policy and didn't want any roadblocks in the new arrangements. When this new phase of our business started in 1967, it was very exciting, and very overwhelming. I was tied to my desk for 5 days a week, and took emergency calls at home on the weekends. Our motto "Have No Fear Empire IS Here" was working, and we were doing a tremendous amount of work.

Empire Used Boiler Supply Company was beginning to get a reputation as a very valuable contractor, and many of the City's complaint problems were being handled in a very expeditious manner. We were available on a 24/7 basis, and we delivered the services. There was an occasion on a Sunday morning, when I got a call from one of the VIP's in the Real Estate Department. There was a TV flash about an apartment building on the upper eastside of Manhattan without heat, and the tenants were demonstrating in front. TV camera people were expected at the building. I was asked to try to help the situation and get the pressure off. I knew that it was impossible to raise a repair crew to get to the building, but I managed to get a truck to the site and have the driver drop lines into the cellar. I gave him instructions to start his welding machine, and let it run while he was in the basement. The TV cameras were on the scene, shortly after the truck arrived, and they saw the welding rig set up, heard the machine running, and the lines were running into the cellar. The mechanic was banging on the pipes, and acting like was doing something constructive. That neutralized the crowd, and they dispersed. The rest of the day was uneventful, and the driver packed up and left at 4 PM. The next morning, the truck returned with a full crew, and repairs were started. I accomplished a very valuable public relations effort, and had defused what might have turned into an ugly confrontation.

My Company was a favorite of the Emergency Repair Department of the City Agency. I was managing a very large operation, and it was proving to be financially favorable. The payment structure was fair, and we were able to pay our subcontractors a fair wage. There was enough left over so that we could manage to show a proper profit. Our subcontractors were happy because we did not pressure them to do our work before their daily first jobs.

The first six months were rough because we were using finance money to pay the contractors. However, as soon as the City finances were in order, the payment checks started rolling in, and it wasn't too long before we paid off our debts to the bank. This fine arrangement was going very well, and when I retired in 1985, I left my brother and his new partner with the operation in progress.

I had made many good friends during those years, and some of them had been elevated to higher positions in the Agency. They were being promoted because we were solving their problems, and we were very happy because we were making a good income from all of that work. Our hard work, and well organized planning, made it possible for us to build a pension, which has been a major part of my comfortable retirement

After several years of wearing the hearing aid, I finally located an Ear Surgeon who would operate to restore my hearing. It was determined that my deafness was a mechanical problem, as the bomb explosion, while I was in New Guinea, had caused a misalignment in the bone structure of my middle ears. The operation was called "stapedectomy", which means removing the stapes from the ear and replacing it with a prosthetic attachment. This proved to be an excellent procedure because, as soon as the operation was over, I could hear buses running down the avenue. I had surgery to both ears, a year apart, and then put my hearing aids in storage. I had regained about 85% of my hearing loss, and could function normally. This was a blessing and life was beautiful again.

While we were living in our 2nd apartment on East 29th Street, I got a call from my cousin Seymour Friedman, who was a wine distributor in Queens. He told me that he was going out of business and had some wine to sell. He had 25 cases of vintage 1974 Cabernet and would sell them for $4.95 a bottle. I bought them all, and got them delivered to my apartment. We stacked them in the coolest place in the basement This was a very fine collection, and I knew that the wine would be a very valuable asset. When we moved up to the house in Otis in 1985, I had a perfect wine cellar. This house foundation was blasted out of shelf rock, and the basement was poured to support the house. The heating and air conditioning system was installed in the basement, with gas for fuel, and we had the benefit of hot air heating, and air conditioning through the ductwork. There were only two houses in the entire community that had this type of system. By the time I left Otis in 1990, and moved to Florida, most of the wine had been consumer, and, in some cases, given away as gifts.

CHAPTER XVII

Mom recovered completely and was back to her normal routine, and the Peskoff household was operating on its regular schedule. My dad, who was usually a quiet and placid personality, began acting badly. He became ornery, hostile and aggressive. He was becoming difficult to control, and after a few weeks of medical consultation, it was determined that he should be hospitalized. He was developing Alzheimer's Disease. When I came to visit at the apartment, I would take him for a walk, so he could smoke a cigarette out in the street. If he smoked in the house, we had to watch him carefully, because we never knew where he would put the cigarette down. He could start a fire, if unattended. He was getting very difficult to control.

I consulted with a local nursing home, which was on the bay and was a very comfortable place to be confined. We agreed to make a substantial monetary contribution for this opportunity and arranged for his physical there. When the Director took me up to the third floor, and showed me the dormitory room that he would be in, I was alarmed. There were no security arrangements. The windows could be opened easily. There were no bars for protection. If my father was in that environment, he would open a window and try to get out. This arrangement was not satisfactory, and we cancelled the request.

We contacted Psychiatry hospitals, and were told that we could bring him out to Kings Point, which was out on Long Island. This was not acceptable, because it would make visiting almost impossible during the week. I spoke to my Political Leader, and he introduced me to the Chairman of the Health Services Department of the NYC Hospital. He told me what he could arrange, and we planned on bringing my father to the Kings County Hospital which was in our area. This Hospital had all the facilities for patients who needed to be confined in a safe, secure facility.

We arrived at the Hospital on a Thursday morning, and my father was examined. He was admitted, and we walked him up to the third floor, and into a ward with eight beds, which had windows which were secured with wired gates. This was acceptable, and we were assured that he would be cared for properly. I made generous gestures to the male nurses, and told them that we would be visiting my father every evening around 6 PM. I hoped that he was cared for properly, and we would be visiting him every evening on the way home from work. Weeks went by, and we visited on a daily basis. Mom brought prepared soups and stews, and he ate ravenously. I'm sure that he wasn't eating the same as when he was home. Mom had recovered completely, and we were resigned to this daily routine. Dad had at least one of us visiting him every day, and we were reasonably pleased. We were sure that he was getting at least one good meal a day.

One morning, I got a call from the floor nurse at 7 AM, and he asked me if I visited my father the night before. I did, and he asked me if I took him home with me because he wasn't in the ward. I couldn't believe what I was hearing. This ward was on the third floor, and in order to get out, you had to go through two gates from the ward to the stairwell. Then you had to walk down three floors, which had gates at every landing. At the ground level there was a gate, which let you into the lobby. The front door was usually locked, with an attendant to give you access. My father had disappeared, and no one knew how he did it.

I called the Police Stations, other hospitals, and even the County Morgue. No one had a positive answer. Then I called the Kings County emergency ward, and asked them if they had a John Doe in the ward. The nurse told me that they had a new patient, incoherent, in his pajamas, and was brought in by the local police. He was found walking on New York Avenue in his bare feet. This was the end of October, and the weather was foul and blustery. I asked the nurse to lift his pajama shirt and look at his stomach. My father had been operated on three times for ulcer problems, and had three scars across his stomach. When she returned to the phone, she told me that he was identified. My father had gotten out of the ward and the hospital and was walking the streets in his pajamas and was barefoot. He must have been out all night, because he was chilled and was running a high fever. As a result of this escapade, he developed a very bad pneumonia, went into a coma, and he passed away several days later. He was born on October 25th, and he died on his birthday, October 25th. He was 75 years old.

After the funeral, when the household was back to a normal routine, we arranged for my Mom to have a live in companion. We agreed that it was time for Mom to go into a retirement community atmosphere, and we started searching. A new building for Seniors was being completed in Brighton Beach, and since it was partially funded by the State, I had access to a priority appointment. We got the necessary approvals, and Mom moved into 500 Brightwater Court, which was a Senior Citizen building in Brighton Beach, with access to the boardwalk. This was an ideal location, and the family was thrilled. Mom moved into this apartment. It was furnished to her wishes, and she had her caregiver living with her. The four children and their families were in the neighborhood and we were still together. Life went back to is normal schedules. She spent the next ten years here with good friends and constant companionship from her family.

CHAPTER XVIII

I started refereeing basketball games at the local JCH, and also at local church league games. As I progressed with experience, I worked my way into High School, College, and semi-pro games. I was elected President of the Kings County Basketball Referees Association. I was working in the Eastern League semi pros when I had an offer to try out for the NBA League. This was an offer that I could not accept because my responsibilities at Empire wouldn't let me stay away from work. My business was winter oriented and we were in the boiler sales and repair business. I could not take the time away for traveling to the games in remote cities. So refereeing became a secondary part of my past life. I had to continue as a part time official.

Refereeing Eastern League was usually a two game home and home series. My referee partner was a fellow named "Dutch" Garfinkel. We traveled together, and to help with expenses, we sometimes had local ballplayers riding with us for their games. It worked well for us because they helped pay for the gas bills. We traveled from Brooklyn to Scranton, Wilkes-Barre, Hazelton, Sunbury, as that was a hot bed area of Pennsylvania that attracted players who couldn't make it in the NBA. Mostly, the weekends were uneventful, but there was one weekend, which was very memorable.

Scranton and Wilkes Barre were very competitive and hated to lose to each other. We learned that these teams "usually" won on their Home Courts. That made the fans very happy. Their rivalry extended in every sport. Scranton and Hazleton at Hazleton on Saturday nite, drew a large beer drinking crowd, and there was an unusually loud and raucous crowd. This was a very close scoring game, and the ball players were getting unusually rough. We were calling personal fouls very often. We had to call fouls on Scrantons' Center very often, and he fouled out of the game. Scranton fans started hooting and threatening us, and the game ended with Hazelton winning by 3 points. The home team won; and they earned the win. We were hooted, and they were yelling at us. "Wait till we get you tomorrow in Scranton". The coach was so upset that he wouldn't even shake hands after the game, which was the usual procedure. After a few beers and a sandwich, Dutch and I got back to the Hotel and called it a night.

When we got to the Scranton gym on Sunday afternoon, the crowd was ready for us. We were razzed, and we knew that the crowd was ready to pounce on us. The game started with the usual reminders to the players, that we would call them as we saw them. No favoritism was shown to either team. Dutch and I agreed that we would not let anything get away from us and that we would be extremely alert. This was a game to remember. It was rough and tumble from the first whistle. The game was getting rougher and rougher by the minute, and we were calling fouls at every turn. It was at the beginning of the 4th quarter, when the Scranton center, fouled the Hazelton center and then hit him after the foul. I called the personal foul and added a technical foul for the second offense. Pandemonium reigned in the arena. Spectators came down from the stands and the Scranton coach ran onto the floor. "Dutch" called a technical foul on the coach and that turned it into a madhouse. We finally got the crowd quiet, and before we started to play. I reprimanded the coach for allowing this excitement. He threatened us and told us we would never referee in Scranton again. Anyway, the game ended with Scranton losing on their home court. The police escort came and chaperoned us into the locker room. We showered up and dressed and got out of town very fast. Monday's report to the League headquarters explained the weekend circumstances. We were not in trouble with the League, but we never got an assignment to Scranton after that experience. This was the last season for my refereeing, because when I realized that I couldn't accept the NBA offer for the tryout, I would be better off doing something less challenging.

CHAPTER XIX

My workweek was very tiring, and sometimes very stressful. It was a practice that when we had no weekend plans, Dorothy and I would go into the City on Friday nights for a good dinner and a relaxing evening. We were regulars at "Nanni's il Valetto" restaurant on East 61ˢᵗ Street, just off Lexington Avenue. This was a basement restaurant in an old brownstone building. We were never denied a table, even though the restaurant was crowded. If we showed up without a reservation, the bartender spotted us, and wherever we were standing, he would find us and hand us our regular Scotch on the rocks. He knew, from past experience, that we would want that drink. It wouldn't be too long, and the Maitre D would pick us out and escort us to a table. He sometimes commented that he couldn't ignore me, but wished that I would call ahead. I couldn't tell him that it was a spontaneous decision, and that I was sorry for his inconvenience. I know that he didn't really mind because I was a very good tipper, and he got a generous tip every time we were there.

It was on a quiet evening after dinner at the Chateau, and Dorothy and I were at the bar, having an after dinner drink. No one else was at the bar, except a little man in a white cook's uniform and the bartender. I pointed to a very interesting Cognac bottle, which was on the top shelf. I asked the bartender what it was, and he told me that it was a very expensive Cognac; Remy Martin, Louis XIV, that was aged fifty years before it went into the bottle. It looked like there were about two drinks left in it, and I asked him what it would cost for me to buy the bottle when it was empty. I told him that I would pay $50 dollars for the empty bottle. The man in the white coat asked me if I was serious, and I said I was. Then he told the bartender to bring out three snifters, and pour three drinks for us. It was then that he introduced himself as the owner, and he said his name was "Nanni". I had never met him before, but I am sure that he knew that we were regular customers. The bottle was empty, and the bartender handed it to me. I put a $50 dollar bill on the bar, thanked "Nanni" for the very nice gesture, and Dorothy and I left for home. That was the beginning of my collecting Cognac. This vintage Cognac is bottled in Baccarat Crystal. Now I was started on another Collectible hunt and would be looking for this vintage Cognac whenever I travelled. I found that this quality drink was selling for about $150 dollars a shot. I recollect that this collection started in 1957.

I even found a bottle in a shop in Cancun when we went ashore from a cruise ship. During the next fifteen years, whenever we were on a trip, I would accumulate another twelve bottles of Napoleon Cognac in Baccarat Crystal bottles. We traveled to St. Thomas and I found one. We found another in a duty free shop in Hawaii. In a small shop in Puerto Rico, we found another bottle that was coated in dust. The owner just stabbed at a price and I bought it. I even found one in Cancun in a shop where you would least expect to find such a buy. The only Baccarat not a Cognac is a Bourbon in Baccarat that I bought in Brooklyn, in my local liquor shop.

I am certain that any Cognac in Baccarat Crystal that is bought today would cost in excess of eighteen hundred dollars a bottle. My entire collection of 12 bottles cost me less that $150 dollars a bottle. The collection is now wrapped and stored in a closet, and I am looking to find a collector who might be interested in buying the entire collection.

CHAPTER XX

I was invited to join the local 42ⁿᵈ A.D. political club by one of my neighbors who was the New York State Senate representative from our district. His name was William Rosenblatt. He was a very gentle soul, and was always making the annual donation appeals at our Synagogue. He was an eloquent speaker and got good results. City Councilman Charles Schumer was one of our local aspiring politicians, and we helped foster his ambitions. He is now a U.S. Senator from New York. Over the years, working with the leadership, I met and worked with many of the men who run the engines of our New York City machinery. I never wanted any political positions. All I wanted was to help those that wanted to get ahead. That worked well with the membership. I wasn't going to be competition, so they fully embraced me, and accepted all the help I could give them. It helped me also because I was able to get temporary summer jobs for my neighbors' kids. Being in the loop was a very enjoyable position.

At one time, one of my dearest friends asked me to try to get her son accepted into the Secret Service. This was a very big favor, but I tried. I spoke to my friend, "Chuck" Schumer, who was then a Congressman from our District. Paula's son was accepted and was sent for training in Virginia. When I returned from a vacation several months later, I asked her how her son was doing. She was very embarrassed and told me that he had "flunked out" and was sent home. I asked her what happened, and she told me, "he failed machine gun". It seemed that he could not hold the gun steady, which was a very important requisite. The secret service couldn't tolerate any inexperience. Their job was to protect the President of the United States at any cost, including danger to themselves.

Everything was going along very smoothly in my life. Business was improving, and we were getting involved with the NYC Building Department, and doing work in rehabilitating old buildings with heating problems. I was totally adjusted to the hearing aid improvement for my hearing problems. Ellen was going to be married, and all arrangements were being made. I suddenly became unsteady on my feet and had lost some of my equilibrium. I was diagnosed to have an inner ear infection and had to be hospitalised for emergency surgery. I had to have an emergency operation in the left ear to cure the problem. The end result was a total loss in the left ear, as the nerve was dead, and I could never have any hearing in that ear again. This meant taking the hearing aids out of storage, and making them part of my body again. The only difference was that the left ear aid was being used as a transmitter, sending the sounds across to the right ear, which still had most of the hearing capacity. Now I knew that I would have to use hearing aids forever. I could live with that and was perfectly adjusted to the lifestyle again. When Dorothy called the Doctor to find out how I was, he remarked that I was very lucky because I was Jewish. The infection was running from right to left instead of left to right. If it was the reverse, my brain could have been involved, and that would have been fatal.

I became an Officer in my Men's Club, and was a member of the building committee. I got more involved in the daily activities of my Congregation. The expression, "find a busy man, and you will find an active worker" applied in my case. I became the Men's Club President, Congregation President, and then Chairman of the Board. Not at the same time, but in progression, as the years rolled on. All of this, and more, as I got involved with the Social Committee, which was planning on doing amateur Broadway at our Temple.

One evening, I got a call from the President of the Sisterhood, Faye Oxman. She invited Dorothy and me to go to the Westbury Music Center with another couple to see a play called FIORELLO. Harry and Rose Diamond were the other couple. After the show, while we were having coffee at Senior's restaurant, Faye asked us how we liked the show. We all loved the show, and told her so. Then she said, "OK, which one of you will take the lead in the show?" Sisterhood was going to produce the show for the Congregation, as a fundraiser for the Temple. Neither Harry nor I had acted before, and Harry immediately declined. Then she turned to me and asked me. Dorothy said I should do it because I had a little resemblance to LaGuardia. I had no acting experience, but the challenge was thrown at me and I accepted. Shortly after that, we went into rehearsal. The next three months were very intense. Work all day, and rehearse all evening. Memorizing lines and learning to sing was very challenging. I was into this show with all my interest and exuberance. I wanted it to be a success. I learned the part well and was ready for opening night.

We had rented the Sheepshead Bay High School auditorium for three consecutive Saturday night performances. Broadway was coming to Brooklyn. We had a sellout of 990 tickets for each of three performances. Opening night, with a full house, and a six piece orchestra, the curtain went up.

As the curtain started up after the overture, and I walked on stage, across the back, to my office, and hung my black fedora on the coat hanger, I became overwhelmed. I turned towards the audience, and started to walk down stage to say my first lines; the entire audience was standing up and applauding and cheering.

"Fiorello LaGuardia" was reincarnated. The overwhelming applause threw me for a loop. I couldn't get a word to come out. I was mumbling and stuttering. My mind was blank. So, I turned my back to the audience, and moved around with all of the gestures, while my secretary was throwing lines at me. I was gesturing and incoherent, as the scene ended, and we went off stage. I was in a panic for a few seconds. Then, I got my composure back, returned for my next scene, and was letter perfect. The show ended to standing ovations for the entire cast. Opening night was a real success. The rest of the week was a real ego lifter. Everyone in the neighborhood started calling me Mr. Mayor. The way I was being treated, I could have sold my autographs. Now, I was beginning to act like a professional actor. I couldn't wait till the next performance.

On the night of the 2nd performance, I was cool and collected. I walked across the stage, hung up the fedora and turned to the audience. As I walked down stage, to the standing ovation, I was cool and relaxed. I waited for the audience to stop applauding and sit down. Then, I started my lines, and the performance went through till the end with letter perfect precision. The second night was another beautiful success. The third performance was a repeat of the first two, and the cast had a lot to be proud of.

We wrote to Mrs. LaGuardia, and asked her if she would attend our final performance. She accepted, and was introduced from the stage. When the performance was over, she came back stage to congratulate us. That was the best part of the entire production. She was very kind, and appreciated the effort that we had undertaken. We did a great acting job, and she was glad to have been a witness. We were ecstatic and grateful for her kind comments.

At our cast party the following weekend, we announced the final results. We had turned in approximately 15,000. dollars to the Congregation. The Beth Shalom Players were now something to be reckoned with. We would regroup and continue with another production.

It took us about a year to get over the success of Fiorello, and some of us were getting anxious to try another show. Now that we had the first show under our belts, we felt more confident, and more professional in our attitudes. We learned from the first shows missteps, and didn't want to make the same mistakes. We called a meeting of the group, and Fay Oxman started proposing options. Someone mentioned doing "Milk and Honey", which sounded interesting, and the group decided to give it a shot. Suddenly, I had a great thought, and saved it for a meeting of the group. When we were assembled and in discussions, I popped up with a great idea. Since we had agreed to do Milk and Honey, I was going to propose someone for the lead female role. I was going to propose naming Faye Oxman to play the lead female role of Molly Picon. It was a sudden surprise and fully accepted by the group.

Faye couldn't say no, and that lead role was settled. The ball was rolling and we put our committees together. We got the OK from

Tams Widmark, who had the rights to the script, and we got our copies for the case members. We were on our way to another fund raising project.

Now the roles were reversed. I became the Producer, and Faye was the leading actress. We started rehearsals before Christmas in 1964, and hired David Jaffee to do the directing and act as Musical Director. We set the opening for March 13, 1965, and included the following two Saturday nights for the other two performances. Sheepshead Bay High School was our theatre again. We priced the tickets at the same five dollar level. Everything went as scheduled, and the cast was fully prepared. I played a small role, portraying a young fellow who eventually married the girl he made pregnant. The wedding ceremony and the "hora" dance afterwards were the hits of the show.

We ran through the three performances to sell out crowds again, and turned the profits over to Beth Shalom. At the cast party, which we held at the Synagogue, we donated another $15,000 dollars. Not bad for a bunch of amateurs. We worked very hard for three months of hard rehearsing. Success had a very uplifting feeling for us, and we felt that we had completed a very rewarding effort. Basking in the glory of a second winning performance gave us added courage, and we were going to embark on a third venture.

I accepted the challenge to produce a third show in 1967, and, after the two previous efforts, I was feeling like a real professional. I was going to do something spectacular if I could get the support of the crew. I huddled with Herman Harper, my right hand assistant, and Jerry Pogostin, our Stage Manager. We agreed to attempt "How to Succeed in Business Without Really Trying". This show had run on Broadway, and proved to be a very successful presentation. We went to Tams Witmark, and got the OK and the script and arranged for Sheepshead Bay High School for the 3rd time. We set April 1st, 1967 as the first of 3 Saturday nite performances. The logistics were all in place, and we contracted with David Jaffee for this show. He would be our Pianist and Musical Director.

When we had our first conference with our Director, Dave Jaffee, we saw a major problem arising. He told us that this cast required six young women to be the secretaries who could sing and dance, and most importantly, they had to be thin and nice looking. This was a major decision for us. We were going to face the Sisterhood and have to tell them that we would have to look elsewhere for these members of the cast. Our members couldn't fit the part of singing and dancing secretaries and be believable.

It was our policy to give our Director control of approving the actors for the shows, and this is what he wanted. He was the Professional and we were the amateurs. We knew that we were in for a rebellion. When we told Fay Oxman that this was the decision, and she was part of our group, she had the mission to deliver the facts to the Sisterhood women. There was a great deal of anger and disappointment, and the message back to us was," there would be no cooperation from the Sisterhood, and we would have to look elsewhere for female players". This was a serious split after two successful ventures. We held to our position and started casting.

One of our lead actors, Phil Barenfeld, who was a surgeon at Maimonides Hospital, and since he was to be the lead role in the show, we imposed upon him to find us six (6) secretaries amongst his nursing staff. It took 2 weeks to assemble a cast, and we set up an intensive rehearsal schedule. We had just celebrated New Years Day 1967, and we wanted to have opening date on April 1st. At the next meeting of the Production staff, we decided to go for broke, and set the ticket price at $10 dollars. We were very ambitious, and felt that we could do a really professional job of presenting this play. We really wanted to make this show a great adventure and a financial success.

Jerry Pogostin, our Stage Manager, suggested that we go all out with the reality of the show, and build a scaffold to be used for the opening of the show. If you can remember the opening, on Broadway; the curtain came up with a spotlight on the lead actor coming down from the proscenium, on a scaffold, which was being lowered from the top of the proscenium. He sat on the scaffold, holding the book; reading from the title, which said,

"How To Succeed Without Really Trying". This was his recommendation, and we worked on it successfully. We built the scaffold, and made it work. We went to the school prior to the show schedule, and were allowed to set up the scaffold, to see if it would work properly. The custodial staff was very cooperative, and allowed us to store the scaffold there for the few weeks prior to the show dates. The cast was in rehearsal, the logistics were in place, costumes were being made for the secretaries and dancers, and we printed the tickets with the $10 dollar price tag. We contracted for the playbill, which was paid for from advertising proceeds. Now we had to start selling the tickets. We were faced with almost three thousand tickets, and we couldn't expect to ask the Sisterhood to help with the sales. We had to be creative, and find other areas for potential sales. Dr. Phil Barenfeld took care of the hospital potential sales and that was successful. I took care of the local Political Club, and my friends were very helpful in selling tickets to the local politicos. With a real strong sales effort, we managed to sell more than 2700 tickets, covering the 3 performances. We went over the top in every aspect of this venture. So much so, that after opening night, when the Sisterhood women saw the effect the young pretty secretaries had on the audience, they reluctantly accepted the fact that we did the right thing. They relented, and even bought tickets for the 2nd and 3rd shows. Each performance ended with the scaffold being pulled up, with the lead on the scaffold, reading the book, before the curtain closed.

This endeavor was another total sellout effort, and when we had the cast party at the Temple, we invited the entire Congregation to be a part of it. The Sisterhood got a special invitation, which they accepted. It was a fabulous evening, and during the festivities, we donated a check for $25,000.dollars to the Congregation President

CHAPTER XXI

Business at Empire Boiler Co. was increasing, and we were able to get summer vacations whenever we wanted. Dad owned the business, and Simon, Herb and I could take time off, as there was very little pressure, when there was no demand for heating. Summer time was spent mostly in reconditioning inventory and getting merchandise ready for sale and delivery in the winter, when the furnaces were operating. This was normal routine every summer. Our work force was very capable, and they were good and loyal employees.

We were told about a hotel in Lake Huntington, upstate New York, called Green Acres, where vacationers were usually from the school systems and people who liked cultural entertainment. We decided to try it for our first summer vacation when Ellen was 4 years old. It turned out to be a very good choice because this was a repeat summer vacation trip for the next 3 years.

When we were taken to our room, we found the neighboring people to be very friendly. The Schultz family was vacationing next door. Herb and Dorothy Schultz became good friends. The hotel owner was Rose Rosenberg, a widow, whose daughter and son in law ran the operation with her. "Cissie" ran the Office, Larry was a part time baker and maintenance supervisor, and Rose was the kitchen manager.

Rose owned a parakeet and often let if fly around the lobby to amuse the guests. Ellen loved that bird, and was always petting and feeding it tiny grain tidbits. All she had to do was put out her hand, and the bird would fly to her. Rose asked her if she wanted to give the bird a name, and she responded by saying she would call him "Elmer". Elmer was a good idea because her late husband's name was Elmer, and she did not object to this pretty bird being given her husband's name.

On Sunday mornings, after breakfast, it was customary for the guests to sit around the lobby, discussing the current events. With my hearing problem, I found it difficult to join in these discussions because I couldn't keep up with the constant cross talking. My routine was to sit off on a side and tackle the NY Times crossword puzzle. I worked with pencil because I did a lot of erasing at that time. On this one particular Sunday, I had been very successful, and had most of the puzzle solved. I went back into the lobby, and when I saw Ellen playing, I gave her the paper to play with. I gave her a ballpoint pen to scribble, and left her sitting on the couch with her legs crossed, and working on my completed puzzle. She was writing over my penciled in letters and redoing all of the boxes in ink. One of the older women was passing, and said to me, "I didn't know your daughter was a genius, and she can do the puzzle in ink". I had to explain that Ellen was good with crayons, and could do very well in copying and tracing, so letters were just a part of what she could copy. As it turned out, Ellen did become very talented, and became the Secretary of the local Mensa Society in Brooklyn. This is a group of very intelligent people with a very high IQ.

Part of the "Green Acres" activity staff was a small three piece orchestra that provided the music for the evening entertainment. The musicians were full time staff, and we became very friendly. Al Arkus was the pianist, and Murray Kaplan was the saxophone player. He had a girl friend named Jan Auster, who was a neophyte composer, and she was working on a song called " Mommy Darling". I told her about the song I had written the lyrics for, and then I began working seriously, on composing the music. It was late in August, the first year at this Hotel, that I had completed the music, and was polishing up the rough spots.

Jan loved the lyrics, and when I played the rough version of my melody, she told me that we should have it worked on by a professional arranger, and then have it recorded at a Demo Studio. I agreed, and we started to search for someone to complete my project. Al Arkus knew an arranger named Sidney Green, and I called him for a consultation. We met, and I gave him my draft of the music, as I had written it on music paper. He took it from there. When he called me, and we arranged to meet, he gave me a finished lead sheet, and an orchestration copy of what could be used to pull the parts for each instrument in an orchestra. This composition was a real professional piece of work, and I was very proud to see my name as the composer.

Al took the music to a demo studio and had a vocalist study it. When she was ready, the studio recorded her singing my song "One Careless Moment", with Al Arkus as the pianist. This demo session produced a recording on an audiotape and a 78 rpm record. The vocalist was a talented singer named Ginny Gibson. Now, I had a complete set of finished works, including a record, a tape and sheet music to brag about.

My cousin Harold Friedman, who lived in Westchester, NY, had a neighbor named W.C. Handy, who was the composer of "St Louis Blues". We arranged for me to meet him, and to show him my music. When we got to his home, we were introduced to him and his companion. Mr. Handy was blind, and his caregiver was also his piano accompanist. When she finished playing the music, Mr. Handy's remarks were very complimentary. He told me that the music was good, and the words were very meaningful. However, he didn't think that the song could be promoted. It didn't have any commercial pizzazz. I wasn't upset because I just wanted an opinion and not someone to tell me that he would publish it. I wasn't interested in becoming a Composer. I love the song, and I play it often. It brings back some memories of a part of my life that helped me mature.

When this summer vacation was over, we all went back to our respective homes in New York City, and resumed our regular lives. We continued to spend time with the Schultzes. One of the first things Ellen asked when we got to our apartment, was for me to buy her a parakeet, and we saw a parakeet in a local pet shop. We bought the parakeet, and a cage to house the bird, and always kept the cage on the top of our piano. A few years later, I came home one afternoon, and found the bird on the floor of the cage, belly up. Ellen was crying, and I said that we could bury the bird in the back yard, and plant flowers over the grave. Ellen said NO, and that she wanted to keep the bird in her bedroom. I had no choice, so we found a taxidermist, and had "Elmer" stuffed. He was mounted on a branch, and looked alive, as he was perched under a pretty glass shell. Fifty five years later, Ellen has a home in Florida today, and "Elmer" is still sitting under his glass shell, on display in her den, and he looks like he is ready to leave his perch and fly around again.

CHAPTER XXII

I was initiated into the Masonic Fraternity in 1957, and was attending my first vacation weekend with them in Atlantic City. Our hotel had access to the boardwalk, and it was customary for us to walk around seeing the sights. I had our dog McDuff with us, and was parading him on the boardwalk. I had trained him to walk off leash and to heel, and he was very obedient. When I stopped, he stopped, and immediately sat at my heel. When I started walking again, he jumped up and joined me step for step. Passers by were amazed at such an obedient pet. If I stopped at a corner, he would sit at the curb and wait for a command to cross. When I saw that it was safe for him to cross, I would clap my hands, and he would run across the street and sit on the curb, waiting for me to get there. He was truly a remarkable animal and a very loyal pet friend.

I made a stop at a window of a shop that was selling porcelain objects, and spotted a miniature Scotty figurine in the window. When I went into the store, I tied McDuff to the gate with his leash, and he sat patiently. The figurine I saw was a Plaster of Paris Scotty, with a price tag of one dollar, and I bought it and looked around a little more. Then I saw a Royal Daulton Scotty, curled in a sitting position. It had an eight dollar price tag on it, and I bought it too. Then the owner showed me another piece, a Scotty upright on his hind legs, in a begging position. I bought that for eight dollars also. On my way out of the store, with my purchases, I passed a cabinet that had a little Scotty, made of twisted wiring. I asked the owner for a price, and he said 40 dollars. I said thanks, and left the shop. I unleashed McDuff, and continued my walking. I was about a block away, and decided to go back to buy the wire

Scotty. When I entered the shop and asked the owner to sell me the piece, he said "you're too late; it's walking out the door now". Someone else had bought, what turned out to be a gold wire collectible, which was a very valuable collector's item.

Then I realized that I had missed a very good buy, and resolved never to let it happen again. This was the start of a very large collection of Scotty miniatures. In all the years of my collecting, which started in 1957, I had accumulated more than 275 miniatures, in every form of composition. My collection included most every porcelain manufacturer. Some were made of coal, wood, glass, jade and ivory, and even solid 14 carat gold, which I had cast from a pewter model, and a gumdrop, which I found in a confectionary store. I still have the molds in my possession.

My most valuable piece was a Royal Daulton porcelain, showing a "flapper" sitting on a garden bench with her legs crossed, a Scotty on her lap, and a Scotty at her feet. This piece had been listed in a catalog for fifteen hundred dollars. I had bought it early on in the buying years, sight unseen, from a dealer in London, for three hundred dollars. The other most valuable pieces were an ivory, hand carved free standing Scotty, a free standing Scotty etched in Jade, and the solid 14 carat gold free standing Scotty.

I was a member of the "Wee Scots" collector's club, and had some of my pieces shown in one of the magazine issues. When the dealer saw the magazine, and my display, he called me, offering to buy the "Scotties" piece. He was very insistent, and I finally agreed to sell. However, I told him that he would have to buy the rest of my collection. I told him that I would put all of the items on a video, with a line item for each, and he would have to make an offer for at least 200 pieces. Then I mailed him the video and the itemized sheets, describing each piece.

A week later, I got a call telling me that he was sending me his offer in writing. He had itemized the pieces that he wanted, and would be very appreciative if I would consider his offers. When I got his letter, I found that he had itemized more than 225 pieces, and the prices were right. He had agreed to give me the fifteen hundred dollars for the " Scotties" piece, and asked me to reduce the asking price for the gold, jade and ivory pieces. He was offering one thousand dollars for each of the three pieces. I talked it over with Dorothy, and we agreed that we would sell. Every price that he had offered was better than I had expected, and the grand total exceeded twenty-seven thousand dollars.

My buyer was driving to Florida from Illinois, and would pick up all of the pieces when he got here. He arrived in a four door sedan, loaded with all types of packing material and boxes to carry everything back home with him. It took him 4 hours to pack and box the entire purchase, and when he left, he gave me 2 checks for the full amount.

I still show two of my favorite pieces. One is an etched inverse Scotty head, which was etched from a picture of my McDuff, and the other is an etched whale tooth, mounted on a teak box. The tooth has a picture of McDuff etched into the side. This piece has a very interesting history. We were on a vacation to Kennebunkport, Maine, and saw some very interesting scrimshaw etchings. I asked the owner if he could etch a dog head on one of his ivory pieces. He said it was illegal to sell whale's teeth. Then I pointed to a little teak box that I wanted to buy, and the price was very nominal. I asked him what he would charge to etch my dog's picture on another saleable item, and he said 150 dollars. The box was 25 dollars, and I said. "Okay", sell me the box for 175 dollars and give me the etched whale tooth as a gift. That way you wouldn't be breaking any law because you wouldn't be selling me the tooth. He laughed, and finally agreed. The teak box, with the tooth glued on the lid, is sitting on my piano today.

The inverse etching of McDuff, in Lucite, has an interesting story. We were vacationing in south Florida and passed this little shop, which showed samples of his process of inverse etching. I showed a picture of McDuff to the artist, who was wheelchair bound, and asked him to etch the picture on a Lucite block. I wanted to show it as a standup showpiece. He agreed, and the price was settled. He would charge me 75 dollars, and that was fine. As we were leaving the shop, I saw a six inch square block of Lucite on display, and the subject was the Garden of Eden, showing Adam and Eve, and the apple tree with the snake, all of which was etched internally, through a little hole in the bottom of the Lucite. It was magnificent, and when I asked him what it would sell for, he said he might sell it for one thousand dollars. The following year, on another trip South, we visited the same shop. When we went inside, there was a new owner. The former owner was a very sickly man, and had died. I asked about the Adam and Eve piece, and was told that it was sold, and on display in an Art Museum.

I was visiting my friend, Herb Schultz, in his office, and while I was at his desk, he pushed a piece of metal towards me and said, if you can pick it up with your fingers, without sliding it, you can keep it. I couldn't pick it up, even though it was no larger than a Hershey chocolate bar. He told me that it was a platinum bar that weighed 6 pounds. Then we got down to business, and I told him what I would like. I found a gumdrop that looked just like a side view of a scotch terrier, and would like to have a gold casting made. I also brought a miniature pewter Scotty that I wanted to have done also. Herb was in the casting business, and did the casting for diamond engagements rings, and other types of rings. He agreed, and told me that all I would have to pay was the cost of the gold. When he gave me the finished products, all I had to pay him was $200 dollars for the weight of the gold.

I took this pendant to my jeweler, and he added a white gold choker, embedded with diamond chips, and sapphire eyes. The gold Scotties were then polished and looked gorgeous. Wherever Dorothy wore that neckpiece, it was a talking point. No one had ever seen such a beautiful pendant. The other miniature piece was added to my collection of Scotties.

We made arrangements with the Shultzes for a vacation week at the Mayflower Hotel on Cape Cod, Massachusetts. When we arrived, it was a rainy Friday afternoon. There was nothing we could do on the outside, so we meandered around the lobby. We didn't talk to any of the other guests because no one was making any overtures to be social. Every one was very aloof, and I thought that we were being snubbed. I told Herb that if this kept up, and the rain didn't let up, I wanted to go home. When we came down for breakfast, the activities director announced a "hole in one" contest. The rain had stopped, and the sun was out.

When we got to the golf area, there were about 20 people who were going to compete. I signed in and waited for my turn. Each contestant was to have three tries to hit a golf ball about 125 yards to the green. The closest to the pin would get the prize. I was a fairly accurate golfer, and played in the low 90's, so it didn't pose too much of a problem. When I was called to come up, I relaxed, gauged the distance and took a 5 wood as my choice of club. I knew that if I hit the ball right, I could reach the green with no problem. All I had to concentrate on was to hit the ball straight. My first shot was perfect, and flew straight as an arrow. It landed about 7 feet from the pin, and ran up to the cup, stopping 3 inches from the hole. My 2nd and 3rd shots weren't as successful. However, when all of the contestants had taken their shots, I was the closest to the pin, and I was the winner. After lunch, the Athletic Director called me up to the front, and presented me with the statuette, which was the first prize. When we went into the lobby after lunch, many of the guests congratulated me, and were completely different from the preceding evening. They were cordial and sociable, and we had a very pleasant vacation from then on. I didn't realize that New Englanders were very reserved and not as openly friendly as the New Yorkers. This was another lesson learned.

The Schultzes became very good friends, and we were very compatible. We did a lot of traveling together. We planned a week at the Concord Hotel in upstate New York. Herb was a good Gin Rummy player and had friends who were regulars at the Concord. He had a defect in his left leg, which made it a little shorter than the right leg, and as a result, he was limited in his physical activities. He planned on playing cards, and I was arranging to play golf for the week. We would let the women do what they wanted to do during the day, and after dinner we would watch the shows. That was the format when you were in the Catskills.

I had the suitcases packed, and in the car, when I left for work that Friday morning. I had arranged for Dorothy to take a cab downtown, and we would drive to the Schultzes, leave our car there in his garage, and go up together in their convertible car. Dorothy called me around noon, and told me that Dorothy

Schultz had told her that she didn't want to leave her daughter Carol at home alone. She was begging off the vacation. Then Dorothy called me and said that if Dorothy Schultz wasn't going, she didn't want to go either. This proved to be a big dilemma.

I had made golf dates with my foursome, and Herb had made dates with his cronies for the gin games. If I defaulted, that would create a bad impression, and spoil a golf week for my foursome; and Herb didn't want to cancel either. We decided to bite the bullet, and tell our wives that we were going with them or without them. I had never gone on any previous holiday without my wife, and this would be a first. I told Dorothy that Herb and I were going to go on our own, and I would be home the following Sunday.

I must admit that this week was a very full week of activities. I played golf every morning, spent the afternoon around the pool making matches for the single guys and gals. I was acting like an unpaid Social Director, and I loved every minute of it. We sat at the singles table, even though we both wore marriage bands. We weren't flirting, but we told the single women that if they couldn't find dates for the evening activity, they could join us at our reserved table in the nightclub. Herb got VIP treatment and got special privileges from the staff. We were having a great vacation. Every evening, after the show was over, I would ask Herb what to do, and he said "let's get some coffee and go to bed". The vacation was over, and driving home was routine and uneventful.

When I got home and greeted Dorothy, I was very emotional and happy to be home. I told her that the week was very eventful, but I didn't like the idea of her not being with me to enjoy the time together. I didn't think that I would ever do that again. There was a time when I was away by myself on a business trip. But that was a necessary trip because I was selling 175 space heaters that were used on a new construction site and were obsolete parts to be disposed of and sold.

I spent a week traveling from NYC through Connecticut, into Massachusetts and then into Pennsylvania, soliciting some of our customers. This was a five day venture, and I called home every evening after dinner. I didn't like motel life at all and spent about an hour on the phone every night before I went to sleep. The trip was successful, and all 175 space heaters were allocated and sold. After all was said and done, the traveling experience was a good one because I finally met many of the customers that we only spoke to on the telephone. We kept a good relationship until I retired in 1985. One thing was certain, and that I wouldn't want to travel alone if I could avoid it.

We found out about Trail's End Camp from the Schultzes, because their two kids were going there for the summer vacations. The owner, Joe Laub, was a very conscientious person, and the campers were afforded quality care and consideration. He ran a first class camp operation. He proved it to me when he asked me to go up and see the camp before we signed a contract. When I returned to NYC after visiting the camp, he called me and told me that he had to build a new bunkhouse to accommodate Ellen and a few other kids. When he asked me what kind of mattress Ellen slept on and I told him foam rubber, he told me that he would order all foam rubber mattresses for that bunk.

I later found out that his chef was a man who knew food from a child's point of view, and that there would be no wasted exotic cooking. The format was so perfect that there was no watermelon in camp. The reasoning was that the kids would spit the pits on the floor, and he didn't want the mess. His clothing list for each camper was very precise. If you sent extra clothes along, they were mailed back to you collect. On parents visiting days, the dining room would be staffed with outside waiters, so as not to interfere with the camp personnel. When problems arose with special parent requests, he changed the pattern and arranged for box meals to be provided for the parents, and they were served on the picnic ground tables. When Ellen called and asked for a party dress for the final banquet, we called Joe Laub. He then told us not to bother because he was going to set up the banquet for the campers, and tell them that the dress was Camp Whites. He was a very talented and capable educator, and he ran his camp activities for the benefit of the children. There were no special privileges for anyone, including the counselors. Ellen came home and told us that she loved camp tomato soup, which was not on her menu list before she went to Trail's End Camp.

CHAPTER XXIII

In 1967, I was appointed Assistant Camp 7 Chairman; Jessie Heller was the Chairman. He invited me up to see the camp, and Dorothy and I made the trip. We stayed in the Chairman's home, which was a four bedroom house with all of the amenities. It was situated just inside the entry gate to the Camp property, and nothing could pass us without being seen. Each bedroom had its own bathroom facilities and total privacy. We accepted the appointment and agreed to spend the next 6 summers assisting at Camp.

As Chairman, we had the responsibility of hiring the entire Camp personnel, hire the Chef and his kitchen staff, order all the food and prepare all of the menus. We hired a Camp Director and a Camp Mother, and arranged for two nurses on site to staff the infirmary. There was a Doctor on call. This was a completely self-contained operation. We saw all of the bills and authorized their payment. It was a tremendous commitment to make, and we were responsible for the spending of $175,000 dollars every summer. All of this money was raised through a goodly number of fund raising projects. The camp motto was "No man stands so tall, as he who stoops to help a child". This camp stayed in existence for more than 60 years, and we entertained 600 little girls, ages 7 through 11. Each of these girls vacationed with us, 200 at a time for three encampments. There were 10 bunkhouses with 3 counselors in each bunk. Masonic Camp Seven had a complete professional staff. The facilities equaled some of the best private camps that were run for profit.

It was my custom, while I was Camp Chairman, to go up to the younger campers, in their bunks, when it was bedtime. I would tell them little stories, mostly "Aesops Fables" tales. I sat on one of the beds, with the campers all around me and told the stories.

My favorite story was the princess under Spook Rock. This is a story that was based on an old legend that went back to the time when the first Dutch settlers first came to Rockland County. It goes this way.

There once was an Indian princess that was a very beautiful girl. Her father was the Chief of their tribe, and he took care of all of his people. He loved his daughter very much, and was always looking out for her safety. He didn't want any harm to come to her, and his hope was that she would grow up, and someday be the leader of their Tribe. This was during the time that the Dutch settlers were very hostile and attacked the Indians on a regular basis. The settlers usually attacked the Indian camp after dark, so the Chief devised a plan to protect the Princess, and keep her away from any harm. There was a huge boulder at the entrance to the camp, and the Chief dug out a large hole, so that the Princess could hide in it every night. The Chief would cover the opening with a large stone to hide the entrance, and the Princess would be safe. This practice was in effect for many months, and even though the Dutch settlers invaded the Indian camp, they could not harm the Princess.

One night, during one of the raids, the Chief was killed, and no one knew that the Princess was hiding in the cave that was blocked by the big stone. The next morning, when the Indians found their Chief dead, and the Princess gone, they thought that the Dutch settlers had captured her and taken her back to their camp with them. It wasn't until many years later that this story became a legend, and the local residents placed a memorial tablet on the large boulder, telling the story of the Princess. Little did the story teller know that the Princess wasn't captured, but that she was still in the cave under the boulder.

The kids were so excited, that they climbed all over me and asked me to stay until they fell asleep. They went to sleep with the bunk lights on, and when I knew that they were asleep, I left and the counselors turned off the lights. This story is being told mouth to ear because the Bronze plaque on the rock that told this story, was stolen many years ago. The evidence of it having been on the rock is still there because the 4 holes, where the bolts were attached, are still there.

Our dog, McDuff, was the camp mascot, and was a constant visitor up at the camp area. I would let him out in the morning, and he would run up to the Infirmary. He knew that the nurses would give him a treat. He would wait on the infirmary porch until the bugle blew for assembly at the flagpole. Then, he would run down to the assembled campers, and sit with them for the flag raising ceremony. After the flag was raised, the camp marched down to the dining room for breakfast, and "Duffy" would march down with them. He loved being with the campers, and I needed to let the campers know about the dog that was going to be running free among them.

At the first opportunity, when all of the camp was assembled in the dining room, I explained the ground rules about the "Camp Mascot". If they saw him running towards them, there was no problem, as he wanted to play. They could not stop him, but if he stopped where they were, they could pet him, and everything would be okay. It was a perfect understanding, and in the six years we were in camp with the dog, there wasn't an incident.

There was one time when Duffy was at the lake; he came running back for me, and wanted me to follow him down to the edge of the lake. He brought me to a little area that had a nest in it, and purred at the contents. There were four little baby ducklings in the nest. I picked one up and let him sniff the duckling. When I put the little bird back into the nest, he was very happy, and we left them alone. I was amazed that he was so gentle, because Scotties, as a rule, are hunters. There was a very interesting happening about a week later, when Duffy came back to the house, smelling like a skunk. Evidently he was chasing a skunk and got sprayed. I was told that tomato juice would clear up the odor, so I took Duffy down to the lake and gave him a bath in tomato juice. Believe it or not, that did the trick. He smelled like a dog again.

My six summers at Camp Seven will never be forgotten. Dorothy and I loved the responsibility; the Staff was the best; and the campers were all benefiting from our generosity. We provide free vacations for these 600 girls every summer at no cost to their families, and when we returned them to New York City after each encampment, every camper walked off the bus with a brand new dress, which was donated by one of our members who was in the clothing business.

There were no secrets kept from me during my years at Camp. The Counselors were girls whose ages ran from17 to 20, and their indoctrination was given to them during the three days prior to the camp opening.

I had four rules that could not be broken without a penalty.

1. THERE SHALL BE NO HITCHHIKING ON ROUTE 59, UNLESS THE CAR WAS A STATE TROOPER"S, OR IT WAS MY CAR.

2. THERE SHALL BE NO 'POT' IN CAMP.

3. THERE WAS TO BE NO SWIMMING OUTSIDE THE CRIB WHEN THE COUNSELORS WERE ON DUTY. ANY COUNSELOR FOUND IN THE WATER OUTSIDE THE CRIB HAD TO HAVE AN EXCUSE THAT SHE FELL IN BACKWARDS OR WAS PUSHED.

4. ALL BATHING SUITS WERE TO BE OFF WHEN THE GIRLS TOOK SHOWERS. THE COUNSELORS WERE INCLUDED IN THE REQUIREMENT.

When one of the counselors questioned me about the bathing suits, I explained in simple terms, that girls were different than boys because there are a few places that couldn't be reached wearing a bathing suit. After that explanation, there were no other questions.

It was the final Camp dinner at the end of my six summers as Chairman, and the dining room was filled with campers and counselors, and invited Masons and friends. The new Camp Chairman to be, Irving Seidman, introduced all of the guests and those that were going to be speaking. I was being honored for the six years of service. The Camp Director, Eli Gamliel, at the conclusion of his flowery remarks, presented me with a framed hand drawn heart, on which were the signatures of every counselor and staff member. I was astounded and very overwhelmed. I didn't know that this gift was being prepared, and I was not aware of it being circulated. Nothing could please me more than to have such a beautiful gesture given to me by the people I loved to work for and with, for six memorable summers.

CHAPTER XXIV

At a testimonial dinner for me; after serving my term as President of my Congregation for the second time, I was standing at the lectern on our pulpit, looking into the audience before I began my remarks. I looked down at my mother, of blessed memory, who was sitting in the front row of the synagogue. I recalled a time when my mother said, in Yiddish, "zunnele, vie leufs de", which translates into "my son, where are you running".

I turned to her and said, "Mom, you always asked me, where I was running. Tonight, I want to answer that question. There are more than 200 people in this chapel tonight. Most of them, you don't know; but they are my family. You, and the rest of my relatives, are sitting down front. On one side of you are my dearest friends from this Congregation. Behind them are my neighbors from the area. On the other side of you are my Masonic friends, and behind them are my political friends. Sitting behind me, as our guest speaker, is Assemblyman Chuck Schumer, who has been my friend for many years. You all are my family. "I have been running to be with my family". I couldn't say it any better. That was my entire speech. Everything that I had prepared to say became incidental, and that was my response to the audience for such a splendid turnout. With that, my Rabbi Fink called my mother up to the altar, and she put the Tallith around my shoulder. That was my Congregation's gift to me as the outgoing President.

A few years after my Dad passed away, my mom relocated to a very comfortable high rise apartment building in Brighton Beach. The location was perfect, as one of the entrances led out to the Boardwalk. We engaged a full time aide, as she was having difficulty in walking and used a wheelchair. This was a perfect environment for her, and she made many new friends in her building. There were regular "kalooky" card games in their apartments, and parties in the social room in the basement. Her aide, Ursula, was very devoted and caring, and mom was very comfortable. On the occasions when we took mom out for dinner, Ursula went with us, and got used to eating American style cooking. She didn't want to use the wheelchair too much, so most of her card games and gatherings were in her apartment. That worked out perfectly, as Mom was a great hostess.

Everything good was happening in my life, and eventually there was a little glitch. Mom began to fail, and her ability to get around was becoming more and more difficult. This was the beginning of weeks and weeks of constant medical care and lots of medications. Finally, we were forced to have her hospitalized, and we had her taken to Maimonedes Hospital. My sister Shirley was working there as a Public Relations person for the new mothers, and would be able to see her on a daily basis. We visited her every day after work, and we could see that she was slipping away. She finally slipped into a coma, and although she couldn't speak, when I squeezed her hand, she responded to the touch when I asked her to do so. Simon and Shirley were at her bedside with me when I saw the monitor turn flat. Bessie Peskoff passed away, peacefully and quietly. She was finally at rest. Her whole life, as a friend to the world, had ended.

When we were all assembled at the funeral parlor, I was astounded to see the multitude of people who came to pay my mother their last respects. There wasn't an empty seat in the Midwood Funeral Chapel. In fact, the side aisles were filled with standing neighbors and friends. This was truly a tribute to such a lovely and loveable person. After the Rabbi delivered the spiritual messages, I delivered the eulogy, and then some of her organization people delivered their loving remarks. I will include my remarks here, because it tells the whole life story of this wonderful woman.

"In the beginning, GOD made a man and then a woman. For me, the world began with a woman, My Mother. As much as I valued and learned from the things that she did, I valued more, the things that she did not do. She never said NO. She never complained, and she never held a grudge. I've searched far and wide, and never found an enemy of my mother. She saw the good in everything, and even the bad. In her lifetime, she had touched us all. In repose, she continues to bind us together, as we remember her for her tolerance and her strength, her pride and dignity, and above all, for her humor. She will always be remembered for these qualities. Mama was a woman who gave first to everyone and to every cause. Whatever remained was kept for herself. This was her way of life. My first lesson in charity came from my mother. My son, she said, if someone asks you for a dollar, give it! Don't question. Then, if you put your hand back into your pocket, you will find another dollar. This is a truism that has been a lesson well taught. My mother wasn't the greatest cook in the world (and the congregation broke out in laughter at this statement). But I can remember potato pancakes coming off the 4 burner stove faster than 4 kids could eat them. And in later years, when we were families, faster than all of us could eat them. I remember her aluminum pot, which was on the stove every Friday, with chicken and pot roast for the immediate family; or for a table full of company. It didn't matter how many of us were eating from that pot, there was always enough for everyone to enjoy. Her love was the ingredient that made everything tasteful and fulfilling. This love emanated from her, and we, her children and her entire family, were the benefactors. Not only did we have love, but we also had understanding, and more than anything else, we had the friendship of this most beautiful woman. In health, she was a vibrant and dedicated worker, for all of her interests. Her family was more than husband and four children. It included her brothers, sisters, brothers in law and sisters in law, and all of their children and grandchildren. It included her friends and neighbors and her organizations. She supported Hadassah and Cancer Care, where she was a life member with my sister Shirley and our cousins. She was a life member of Dennis Andrew League for Cerebral Palsy, with my wife Dorothy. She participated with me at Congregation Beth Shalom, when we had our rededication program, after the fire. Her greatest love was the Kaluky players at 500 Brightwater Court and the Pioneer Women. She leaves us a legacy, which is "TO CONTINUE HER WORK".

CHAPTER XXV

T he year was 1984, and I was thinking about retiring from Empire Boiler Supply Company. I was making plans for our future. Ellen was independent in her own right. She was set in her position as Director of Substance Abuse Prevention for Headquarters, New York City, Board of Education. Ellen's future was assured. Dorothy and I had just bought a summer home in Otis, Massachusetts, near Tanglewood, in Lenox, where the Boston Symphony Orchestra spends the summer. We were already commuting up and back on weekends. We were very happy with these arrangements, and looked forward to my retirement. I decided to make June 1985 my retirement year, and that was a year away.

My Masonic friends offered me the opportunity to be appointed District Deputy Grand Master for the 7th Manhattan District. This was a very high honor, and a position I really wanted to have in 1985. Turning 65, retiring from a successful 40 years in business, and being offered the Deputy's appointment, was a tremendous combination of good happenings. I was appointed by the Grand Master, and after installation, a solid year of black tie parties and events were arranged. Dorothy and I were the guests of honor at many occasions, and participated in all the pomp and ceremony that goes with this life. I worked diligently at fulfilling the Deputy responsibilities, and we totally enjoyed this 12 months of activity.

My presentation dinner as District Deputy was held at the top of the World's Fair tower. It was a beautiful Black Tie party, and more than 150 Masonic friends and family were present. As the honoree, it was my decision to name the speakers for this occasion. I limited the speeches to the outgoing Deputy Grand Master and asked

Ellen to be the Guest Speaker. This was a change from the usual program, because I eliminated a lot of speeches that were made by people at most of the other Special Nights. Needless to say, Ellen was very eloquent and spoke brilliantly.

I would do her an injustice if I attempted to write what she said, so I will just insert the speech in its original words, and I quote: "Through the years in Masonry, you've heard my mother quip often that Dad wasn't home very much-that you saw him more than we did-that charitable work was more important to him than family, but as I reflected over the years, I realized that family is of the utmost importance to my father. It's just that his definition of family is broader than most people's. HIS family encompasses all those with whom he comes in contact. I look around this room tonight and I see "family". There are people here who have been part of my life since I was a little girl bagging candy for Camp 7 picnics with Sol Kaiser. I have recipies for mouth watering cakes, (guaranteed not to make you fat) from Sophie and Harold Halper. I have eyeglasses, so I can see you, from Sydelle and Jerry Ivers. I have underwear that even Fredricks' of Hollywood would blush, from Joan and Ronnie Steiner. I've had fabulous vacations, with crummy rooms because, "you only sleep in them anyway, so who cares", from Sam Sternhell. And, while many of you danced at my wedding, a very special "Uncle" Jessie Heller, helped me dance through my divorce. Through my dad's affiliation with you, my family has grown bigger too. When Dad first became a Mason, I thought he was expanding his business, to include construction and masonry. He had that little blue book with the funny writing to study, and then an apron, which you couldn't wear to barbeques.

"Years later, when he was asked to become a District Deputy, Mom wouldn't allow it, until enough lodges merged, so that his dinner obligations weren't larger than his waist size. I was excited because I heard that he'd get a jewel, and I thought that I could add it to my inheritance. He has had the good fortune throughout his life to have touched the lives of others, and enriched them. You know, better than I, the work he's done, both through fund raising and the sharing of his time and boundless energy. However, it was just an abstraction to me, even after many weekends of visiting Camp Seven, until one evening, 2 years ago, I was having dinner during a break between college courses, and I mentioned my father's name. A woman at the table stopped eating, looked at me strangely, and said," your father is Uncle Oscar?" She had been a counselor at Camp 7 many years ago, and she began to recount stories of Uncle Oscar and Aunt Dorothy and "Duffy", her voice filled with love and awe. She felt thrilled to be in the presence of Uncle Oscar's daughter. I was a celebrity!

I spent a good deal of my life resenting the fact that wherever I went, I was simply "Oscar's daughter", but now that I have established my own niche, and have even heard of him referred to as Mrs. Shelton's father, I want to let him know that, deep down inside, I'll always be Daddy's Girl, and being Oscar's daughter has brought me a great deal of pride. Through the years, in his Community work, both politically and in the Synagogue, and in his Masonic work, he has had many titles. People have been honored to call him friend, colleague and brother; but the greatest honor of all is that I get to call him Dad".

Her main congratulatory remarks were over, and then she told a very interesting story, which I will try to recall. The time was when I was President of Congregation Beth Shalom, in Brooklyn. It was a Sabbath morning, during services, when I was presenting the Bar Mitzvah boy with his usual "Kiddush cup" gift from the Congregation. I had walked off the platform, and the Bar Mitzvah boy brought me over to meet his parents. Ellen was with me, and the boy said, "Mom and Dad, I want you to meet Mrs. Shelton's father". That was the crowning point in Ellen's career. Then, she said to the audience at my dinner. "That was the morning when she finally came into her own because all of her life she was living in her father's shadow. That morning her name was used, and I was in her shadow.

CHAPTER XXVI

June 1985 was the end of my connection with Empire Boiler Company. When we came up to the Otis, Mass. area and went house hunting, we were shown many homes on water but they were mostly on stilts, like camp bungalows. We shopped for 4 or 5 weekends, and were about to stop, when a friend of Ellen's asked us to look at one more location. She took us up to the Otis Woodlands, and we saw this house. We fell in love with it and negotiated to buy. We made an offer, left a deposit, and went back to Brooklyn. I told the salesman to call me when the developer came back from his trip. When he called, he said that the owner wanted us to come up for the weekend and discuss the sale.

I had heard that the developer was asking 140,000 dollars for the house, and I left a 10% deposit. When I got back the following weekend, the developer told me that he had someone from Boston, who was willing to give him $168,000 for the house. Then I asked him, why he called me if he could get more money than I offered. I told him that I was ready to buy the house for the 140 thousand dollars immediately, all cash, with no contingencies. I didn't have to live there immediately, and he could stay as long as he needed. His wife had just broken her hip, and was in need of care, so he wasn't in a rush to leave. All he had to do was pay all the bills while he was there. He was silent for a minute, and then he leaned over the table, shook my hand, and told me we had a deal. As part of the deal, I asked him to give me the paperweight, which was on the desk. It was a figurine of an owl. He asked me why, and I said," So I can point to it and say, "this owl cost me 140 thousand dollars". I got the owl, and took it back to Brooklyn with me.

When we left the Office, my lawyer made an interesting comment. He said that this was the first time someone had put it over on Ross Williams in a house deal. I told him that I didn't do anything. All he had to do was say, "split the difference," and I would have agreed. I really wanted the house. The next time I saw Mr. Williams, we went to lunch, and I asked him, "what would have happened if I didn't leave a 10% deposit, when I left after seeing the house?" He commented that I probably wouldn't be talking to him today.

I took occupancy of the house in the middle of November and made plans to be up there for the Thanksgiving weekend, with Dorothy and Ellen, and we would be taking measurements and doing all the things that would be necessary to furnish this house from scratch. It was midweek, and we were staying in a motel in Great Barrington. It was Thanksgiving afternoon, and we were getting hungry. Not knowing that this is New England, and the natives are very proper about Holidays we didn't know that everything would be shut down. Even the gas stations were closed. Restaurants were either booked solid with reservations, or not open. Food was going to be a problem, and I got a brainstorm, and said, I know where we can get dinner. We piled into the car, and drove through town to the Hospital. The cafeteria was open, and we were among the last people to have service. The kitchen was just about out of food. But, we had Thanksgiving dinner, with all the trimmings, for 5 dollars each. And, it really was a very adequate dinner, and we were well satisfied.

Our first venture in Otis was to buy some food for the house, and we stopped at the Otis Egg Farm to stock up. It was a really cold evening, and the weather was below freezing. When we got back into the car, it wouldn't start, as the gas line was frozen. By the time the service truck arrived, we had begun a dialogue with the owners of the Farm, and found that they were the first Jewish family in the town. The farm was started by their Grandfather, and was the first egg farm in the area. The Pyenson family turned out to be very close friends, and we still visit each other on a regular basis.

The first night in the new house was very interesting. We had brought a bridge table and two chairs to the new house, as it was completely bare. The only other thing we had brought into the house was the daily paper. We finished taking all of the measurements that Dorothy wanted, and it was getting late in the day. All of us were getting hungry, and we were thinking of where to eat. Ellen found an ad from an Italian Restaurant in a small suburb, about 12 miles away. The place was named Lagonia's Fire Hill Inn, and we called and made a reservation. We got the directions and started out. As soon as we got into Ellen's Toyota, it started to rain in torrents. By the time we got to Great Barrington, it was almost impossible to see the road, but we kept going. What should have taken about 25 minutes, took more than an hour, and when we got to the restaurant, and parked the car, we got soaked just getting through the front door. The restaurant was deserted, except for the owner and a fellow sitting at the bar. When we told him who we were, and that we came from Otis, he called us nuts, and crazy for coming out in this foul weather. He lived above the restaurant, so he was dry and cozy. The end of the story is that he prepared a very good dinner for us, and sat with us at the table until it was over. We told him that this was our first dinner in the Berkshires, and that we were planning to be regular visitors in the future. When we said goodnight, he made me promise to call him when I got home. He wanted to know that we got there safely. This restaurant was one of our regular dining places for all of the years we were in the Berkshires.

Otis Woodlands is situated in a flyway air pattern, and we often found flocks of Canadian Geese on our open area, taking a break from their flight south for the winter. They were often waddling up to the house, looking for food. I had built an above ground vegetable garden, with a wire mesh fence surrounding it. I was told that vegetable farming was a challenge, and I wanted to prove that I could be successful. There was only a 70 day growing season because of the early cold spells which started after Labor Day in September.

My first effort was to grow lettuce because that was the easiest and the safest. I decided to plant Radicchio Lettuce, from seed, and bought all the necessary equipment to start indoors germination. In

May, the seedlings were ready to put into the ground, and I planted 100 tiny plants. I nurtured this garden constantly, and was rewarded with 100 heads of Radicchio lettuce. All full grown heads, and a very successful project. Now, I had a problem, What was I going to do with all of this lettuce? Since Dorothy and I were very often in the local restaurants, I decided to give each of them some of the heads, and they could serve it to their clientele. That proved to be a very good decision because for many months, we didn't have to buy drinks before dinner. The management was very generous and bought the drinks for us. I never expected such generosity.

The following year, I planted a garden of golden corn from special seeds. I followed the same procedure, from seed to seedling, and then into the ground. That was successful, and the garden was blossoming with tall growing stalks, loaded with ears that were fattening up. One of the weekends in late August when Ellen was visiting, she went into the garden to check on the corn. When she came into the house, she said that the corn would be ready on Sunday, and she wanted to take some home with her on Monday morning. When I went into town for the Sunday morning papers, I checked the garden and was astounded. It seems that the raccoons had the same idea. They were waiting for the corn to ripen, and then they would attack it for themselves. Well, they did a complete job in the garden. There wasn't one stalk left untouched. All of them had been bent over, and every ear was sampled. The raccoons had guessed wrong. The corn wasn't ripe enough to eat, but they killed the crop. The entire project was a wipe out. Every bit of it was transported to the dump. That taught me an important lesson. The next crop would be vegetables that animals would leave alone. The next crop would be tomatoes and Kirby cucumbers. Three years of tomatoes and cucumbers were successful, and many of our neighbors shared in the bumper crops.

My last effort as a gardener was to plan an arbor, which was the base for Kiwi plants. I bought four plants, three female and one male, and planted them at the four corners of the arbor. We stretched wiring across the top of the arbor because these plants grow as a vine, and they would reach up to the wires and wrap around them for support. The only unknown was that I didn't know how long it would take to develop fruit. I learned that it takes 5 months for the kiwi to ripen. I could only guarantee 3 months before it started to get cold, and I was going to see what happened.

After Labor Day, the weather started getting colder, and as the kiwi could not tolerate cold, it slowed the development. I had a fully developed set of vines, with about one hundred tiny little cranberry size kiwis that were not going to get any larger. That was the end of my gardening attempts. We dismantled all of the garden material, and called it a day.

The Woodlands developed into a Community of 200 homes, but it only had about 100 when we bought this house. Most of the owners were NYC educators who used the vacation home during the summer. The area attraction was the Tanglewood Music Center in Lenox, and several Summer Theatre venues in other towns which attracted Broadway talent. The music was the best of any professional orchestras in the country. The theatres performed very excellent plays with name actors and actresses. There were many good restaurants to choose from, and the culture was superb. This was a perfect location in which to take advantage of any or every type of cultural activity.

It didn't take long for us to get acclimated, or make friends in the Community, and we were very happy. I started playing tennis on a regular basis and joined a golf foursome. We had four clay tennis courts, and golf courses were readily available. The Woodlanders were avid sports people, and the tennis courts were being used on a regular basis. We had our pick of golf courses within a ten mile radius of the town of Otis.

The second year we were in Otis, we decided to give up our apartment in Brooklyn and become Massachusetts residents. We registered to vote, traded in the NY license plate and ordered a special plate OWL 78, which was our address in Otis. My connection to New York was all but severed, with the exception being the Congregation Beth Shalom family, whose friendships we still continue.

I got involved with the Community politics, and became a member of the Board. My assignment was to be the Town Liaison, I was active in town meetings. I joined the local Kiwanis Club and became a town activist. The local Volunteer Fire Department asked me to help them raise funds for a new piece of equipment that they wanted to purchase. There had been several accidents on Route 8 on the way up from Connecticut, and they wanted to buy a tool called, "Jaws of Life". This tool was a pneumatic tool that could pry metal loose from the car wrecks, and free people who were trapped inside. They were told that this tool was being used by other agencies, and had proven to help save many lives. I asked our Board if I could solicit our neighbors for this fundraiser, and they agreed to let me do it. I sent letters to all the homeowners, and was rewarded with returns that added up to more than three thousand dollars. This was a great achievement, and the Otis Fire Department bought this very valuable life saving piece of equipment.

During the 10 years that we lived in Otis, we made many friends, and participated in many of the town activities. I bought raffles, as did most of the others in the Community. I won 1ˢᵗ prize in a church raffle and told the committee to give me the cash instead of a bond, and I would give them a check in return. There was another raffle with a food basket as the 1ˢᵗ prize. I was in town for lunch, and the owner of the restaurant told me that I was the lucky winner of the food basket. He showed me a crate, full of boxes, jars and bunches of fresh fruits. I peeled a banana from the hand and told him to give the rest of the produce to some needy people. He told me that there was a 25# box of frozen food also, and I told him to give that away. When I saw the church people who sell the raffles, I told them not to sell me any more raffles. Just ask me for a donation, and I would give them a check. I didn't want to win any more raffles.

I got a call from the minister of the Church, Rev. McKinstry, and he asked me to help him fundraise for the repairs to the Church steeple, which was leaning on a 30 degree angle. They wanted to restore the steeple to its original condition and needed to tear it down and rebuild it. This was to be a very expensive restoration project, and the church needed to raise the funds. I was getting a reputation of being a fundraiser, and the townspeople were asking me to be a candidate for the Town Council. I was eligible to be a candidate, as I was a Massachusetts resident, but I declined. I had enough of politics when I was in Brooklyn. However, I accepted the challenge, and I helped with the fundraiser.

Then I called my friend, Congressman Chuck Schumer, and asked him to get me an introduction to the local Congressman. We didn't have enough money, and we were looking for some kind of grant to help with the financing. When he called me back, he gave me the phone number of the Congressman's secretary, and told me that she was expecting me to give her a call. When I made the call, I was received very cordially, and I made my pitch.

When I finished my presentation, she very politely said to me, "Mr. Peskoff, do you realize that there are 345 churches in Massachusetts, most of them as old as the one in Otis. And they are landmark buildings also. The Government cannot do anything financially for any of the churches because there is a separation of Church and State". However, she was very cooperative and gave me the phone number for a VIP at the Massachusetts Historical Society. With her introduction, and a very well written letter, we were the beneficiaries of a 5,000 dollar check.

Thanksgiving was approaching, and the Congregational Church was planning an Ecumenical Service. Rev. McKinstry invited me to be a speaker, and I accepted. When I told him that I couldn't use the New Testament for reference, he advised me that he could give me a copy of the Old Testament for my information. That worked out fine for me, and I made plans to participate. Thanksgiving afternoon, the new steeple was rededicated. A majority of the townspeople were in attendance. After the dedication, we all were invited into the Church, and the program began. It was a beautiful program, with members of all denominations speaking from the pulpit. Refreshments were served and friendships made the rest of the day a very successful happening.

In 1989 we decided to take a little break, and go to Florida for a month. Ann Marie and John O'Connor had a home in Jupiter at a Condo called Jupiter Ocean and Racquet Club. The agreed to rent it to us for a month, and we drove down. It was a very nice duplex, with a balcony porch and an open loft for the master bedroom. There were two bathrooms, one on each floor. We spent a very delightful month there and decided to see if we could find a similar place to buy. We were very fortunate because there was an apartment for sale, exactly the same as the one we rented. It had the same exposure. It needed complete renovation and decorating, and I told Dorothy not to even look at it. We would contract to have it completely overhauled and painted. Then, when we came down the following winter, she could run rampant, and decorate the interior any way she wanted. I knew that if she saw the place in its present state, she would not want to buy it. I was right, because she agreed and we made the purchase. I called the painter, and Dorothy told him what she wanted to have done. We left for home with the knowledge that the following winter was going to be a busy one. Dorothy had floor plans, and her mind was set on making this new place a very attractive vacation home. She would be occupied all spring and summer, making all of the plans, and cutting pictures from the decorator magazines.

When we returned to Jupiter in the winter of 1990, Dorothy got started immediately, and began furnishing the Condo. The first item was a bed to sleep on, and then everything else happened in proper fashion. It didn't take too long, and the condo was furnished and made livable. We began making friends, and joined in with the Community. When the O'Connor's came south, we joined with them and became regular beach goers at the Jupiter Reef Club, which had a terrace facing the Ocean. We had an opportunity to buy a resale vacation week in the time share program, and became regulars in the Club activities.

CHAPTER XXVII

I got involved with the local Condo politics, and was hearing all the grumblings from my friends about how they couldn't get any changes made to the Community. The existing Board had everything under their control. They had tried to get some of them elected to the Board, but were frustrated because the realtors had a lock on the absentee owner proxies, and nothing could be done.

We organized a group of activists and managed to get control of the Nominating Committee for the forthcoming election. I had studied the documents and found that the Nominating Committee selections were the slate to be presented for election. Any other nominees had to be presented to the Board for inclusion on the ballots.

When the Nominating Committee submitted their recommendations, and the proxies were prepared for submission to the membership, the Board mailed the notices to the homeowners. The night of the election, when we arrived and were handed the ballots, we were surprised to see the Nominating Committee's candidates as the slate, and the three incumbents names listed below as candidates. I knew that this was a violation of procedure but didn't say anything at the time.

When the meeting opened, the person in the Chairman's seat was the Attorney for the Association. When he called for order, I raised my hand and called for a Point of Order. The attorney asked me what the point was, and I asked him if he was a homeowner. He replied that he was the attorney and didn't own a unit. I then quoted from the documents and said that this was the annual homeowners' meeting, and only a homeowner could preside. He sheepishly moved over, and the President took over the chair.

The meeting proceeded in a normal fashion with no complications until it came time for the elections. When the Chair asked to start the balloting, I raised my hand and asked for another Point of Order. When I was recognized, I asked the attorney if this was proper procedure as we were being asked to vote for candidates who weren't on the original circulated Proxy ballots. I advised him that the added names on the ballots disenfranchised owners who were not present at this meeting and couldn't be given a chance to evaluate their names. When the Chairman said that they could be nominated now, and then voted on, I questioned the legality of that judgment. I asked the attorney for his opinion, and when he finally answered, he said that it couldn't be done. The end result was that the election was cancelled and rescheduled for 60 days in the future.

After the rescheduled election, two of the original nominated members were elected, and we had broken the control of the Board. Now we had a foothold in the administration. Jupiter Ocean and Racquet Club had aggressive and homeowner oriented people now on the board and were on their way to a future of proper management.

CHAPTER XXVIII

We were snowbirds for about three years and decided to look around for a possible move into a homeowner community. It was a good thought because we had some friends in a Community called Crystal Pointe, and on a day when we visited with a real estate friend, Linda Newton, we passed a sign on the back fence of a home that said "For Sale By Owner". I asked Linda to go around the front and ask the owner what he wanted for the house. She came back and told me that he wanted $160 thousand for the house.

The property had an enclosed swimming pool, which was in a very large screened in patio. I told her to make the deal. I didn't even want to see the inside because I knew what it would look like, and I didn't want Dorothy to get upset with what she would see if she went in. I had done this before, when I bought the Condo. I knew that a fresh coat of paint would make this place perfect, and Dorothy could do any interior decorating that she wanted. The contract was signed, and we went back north, knowing that the house would be repainted and made ready for use when we came back the following winter.

When we returned the following October, the house had been completely repainted, and the interior was brand new looking, and I knew that Dorothy would be a very happy camper. She hired a decorator, and, between the two of them, they did a beautiful job of furnishing and decorating this new home. I had made a deal with the former owner that allowed him to remain in the house for an extra month during the summer, and he left all of the pool deck furniture for us to have.

We filed for Florida residency and registered our vehicles, and the license plate remained the same, with the exception that it was a

Florida plate and not one from Massachusetts. OWL 78 was now in Florida, and a new life was shaping up.

We made friends very easily and soon became active in Community politics. I worked on the campaigning for two of the candidates for election to our Board, and they both were elected at the next Crystal Pointe Annual election. I went to a Board meeting with a request to install Solar heating on my house so that we could heat the pool. I was told that it could not be done because the panels would be seen from the street, and the documents didn't allow for that. When I challenged their decision and told them that this was an energy saving project, and the County would overrule their decision, the Board questioned my facts. I told them that I was installing the Solar panels, and they could challenge me because I had done my homework and found out that I could do the work. The County rules superceded any documents for any of the homeowner communities. I had proven a very interesting point and made some very good friends when I challenged the Homeowner Board and was victorious. I was elected to our Waterford subdivision Board, and then was appointed to the Maintenance Committee of the Master Board.

From 1985 through 1993, our family had perfect tranquility, and we were very comfortable and happy. We had a full social schedule and developed many friendships. Ellen was a constant visitor, we had week end company whenever we wanted, and many of our Masonic friends were guests. All was perfect, until Dorothy went with one of her friends, to see her doctor. Lillian Barker had Krohn's Disease and was going for a regular checkup. Dorothy was going along for the ride. After Lil had her examination, the doctor asked Dorothy when she had her last check up. Dorothy said that she hadn't seen her doctor in several years and made an appointment for a physical because she had a few complaints during the past several months. The results of the Endoscopy exam showed a suspicion of a tumor in her stomach. A visit to an Oncologist confirmed the suspicion, and we were advised that the tumor could be removed surgically. His recommendation was removal of 2/3 of the stomach, which would remove the tumor and eliminate the Cancer. We agreed to the advice and arranged for the surgery.

CHAPTER XXIX

Dorothy was hospitalized in Pittsfield, and Dr. Faro was her surgeon. The operation was over, and Dr. Faro told us that the tumor was successfully removed, and there was no further evidence of any additional malignancy. The surgery included a bypass around the stomach, as the healing process had to take place. We were told that healing time was about three weeks, and Dorothy would have to be fed through a tube directly into her intestinal tract. The operating team had connected a feeding tube to the intestine, and that was the way we had to feed her. This was not a very complicated process.

The feeding package was connected to a bracket, and the insert was installed, and Dorothy got her nourishment. This was a three times a day requirement, and was not a happy time for Dorothy. She was not in any pain after the surgery, but constantly complained about being nauseous when we were feeding her. Sitting up caused the nausea, so we let her lie down if that was more comfortable. She was a real trooper, and, when she was getting her chemo and radiation treatments, she was very cooperative and managing well.

She lost her hair and wore a bandana on her head. I bought a wig for her to wear, but she refused. She said that if people didn't want to see her bald head, they could close their eyes. She wouldn't wear the wig. I donated the wig to the hospital. Recovery was uneventful, and the chemo and radiation treatments were completed.

The summer of 1993 was over, and we were making plans to return to Florida for the winter. Treatments were concluded, Dorothy was back on real food, and we were getting around socially on a daily schedule. We made arrangements to ride the Auto Train south and had the name of an Oncologist in Palm Beach Gardens. When we got down to Florida, we made arrangements for consultations with the oncologist and settled in for the winter.

The oncologist, Dr Shapiro, recommended a complete MRI scan, so that he could start his own case file. Dr Shapiro was a very kind and understanding doctor, and his office was packed with his patients whenever we came for an appointment. There was a very cute notice in the waiting room that said, "The Doctor gives all of his patients ALL the time they need, so please have patience". I never heard any of the people in the waiting room complain about not being seen on time.

When Dr Shapiro called us in to discuss the MRI, he told us about a little growth on Dorothy's left breast, which had to be removed. That little bit of surgery was completed, and Dorothy went back on chemo and radiation again. His series of treatments were concluded, and another scan showed a little tumor in the right breast. We went through he same routine for the third time. More chemo and radiation, and then a month off, before another scan was taken.

This MRI brought some very distressing news. The scan showed a spot on Dorothy's lung, which was very suspicious. The problem was that it was in a very inaccessible location, and the attempt at surgery would be very challenging. Dorothy decided not to attempt the surgery, and we made plans to go back to Otis for the summer. We arranged for some new injection treatments in Massachusetts and got back to our routine of summer activities.

Tanglewood, was our activity, and Dorothy was a real trooper. She participated in most every activity, and when she was tired, we just did nothing but relax and stay at home. I remember her saying that I should get a caregiver to look after her, and go out and play golf with the boys. She said, "I can afford that." I kept telling her that I could, but even if I did, I would still be there with her. So, "be quiet", and let me do what I am doing.

The summer Tanglewood season was over, Labor Day 1994 weekend was history, all treatments were over, and we were waiting for the Fall Foliage season to begin. We were thinking about heading south for the winter, after the Jewish Holidays. We went to bed in the den, which was where we were sleeping because I didn't want Dorothy to use the steps to go up to our bedroom. I don't know the exact time, but Dorothy nudged me and told me that she wanted to go to the bathroom. Those were her last words. I tried to lift her, but she was dead weight. She didn't respond to anything I said. I called 911, and the ambulance came within 5 minutes. It was in the early hours after midnight.

When the Volunteer Ambulance people got to the house, and saw Dorothy in a comatose state, they called the Pittsfield Hospital and arranged to meet their ambulance in Stockbridge, which was half way from Otis to Pittsfield. Dorothy was put on a stretcher and put into the ambulance. I decided to follow the ambulance in my car because I was going to stay in the hospital with Dorothy. Everything went smoothly, and we met the hospital ambulance as scheduled. Dorothy was transferred to the other ambulance, and I followed it to the hospital in Pittsfield. There wasn't a wasted minute, and everything went smoothly. Dorothy was carried into the Emergency Room and immediately hooked up to the intravenous equipment. She was monitored, and breathing normally. There were no visible signs of motion, but she was comfortable. I was told that the day shift was coming on duty, and they would be bringing Dorothy up to a room as soon as the room was ready.

When we got up to the patient floor, and Dorothy was settled into a hospital bed, I looked out of the window, and it was daylight. All was still, and I got a surprise visit from my personal Internist who was on the floor. He saw me in the room and came in. Dr. Finck didn't say a word, but he put his arm around me and gave me a little hug. One of the nurses came in and checked the monitors, and I told her that I would be staying at the bedside. It must have been about 9 AM, when I noticed that the monitor went flat. I called the Nurse, and she came in and checked. Dorothy had passed away. Her last 14 months were a constant battle with operations and treatments. There was no pain, and she managed the discomforts of the treatments like a real soldier. That was a blessing. Her passing was peaceful, and I was certain that she knew that I was with her until the end. The nurse told me to go home and that they would take care of the arrangements.

I called Ellen and told her the news, and then I called Rabbi Goldfischer and gave him all of the necessary information. He told me that he would make all of the arrangements, and that I should get back to Brooklyn. I went back to the house in Otis, packed a suitcase, and took the three hour drive back to Brooklyn. I called the Midwood Funeral Chapel and found out that Rabbi Goldfischer had already arranged for them to bring Dorothy to Brooklyn for the funeral. When the Funeral Director asked me how I wanted Dorothy to be prepared, I told him to make her look as though she was sleeping.

When Ellen and I went to the chapel that evening, we were pleased with his preparation. Dorothy looked peaceful and beautiful, as if she were sleeping, with her head on a slight tilt. This vision is forever in my memory. I called the mortician and thanked him for such a beautiful preparation. He was overwhelmed, and said that I was the only one who had ever called him to make any comments.

The funeral was on the day before Yom Kippur, and during the Rabbi's eulogy, he remarked, "Dorothy was a very considerate person. She chose to die before Yom Kippur, so that there wouldn't have to be a long period of "Shiva". It is an accepted practice that, when there is a "Shiva" that runs into a Holiday, the period of mourning is excused. We only had the Shiva for one day and then it was Yom Kippur.

I spent the Yom Kippur days at Ellen's apartment, and when we returned from the funeral, one of Ellen's friends had arranged for the refreshments, and had everything ready for us when we got home. That evening and the next day were spent with friends and family, who came to pay their respects. When the company left, and I was ready to get to bed, I was quietly reviewing my life, and I realized that I was alone, and would have to face a new life without my beloved bride of 49 1/2 years. This was going to be a new experience. My major concern was, how do I start a new life alone, and with the thoughts of what will I do, where will I be, and with whom will I be. I needed to refocus on my values, and give serious thought to future planning.

When Dorothy was diagnosed with cancer, I had the realization that she was not going to be with me much longer. She had always joked with me and said." If you die before me, I will kill you". She had been a perfect companion for almost 50 years, and had always put my interests before hers. In her mind, it was family first, in every situation. She had been a more than perfect wife and lover, and a very devoted mother to Ellen. Her respect for our parents was unmatched, and her willingness to be of assistance at any time was foremost in her makeup. She had been my first real love, and will always be in my heart. Her life with me will never be forgotten. She will be a cherished memory until I die. The realization that this part of my life was over made me think deeply about what my future would bring.

Yom Kippur 1994 was the end of my 50 years of a life full of many exciting and rewarding years. I was retired, had a generous retirement pension, owned two homes, one in the Berkshire mountains of Massachusetts, and the other in Palm Beach Gardens in Florida. Ellen was well situated with her position as Director of Substance Abuse Prevention with the NYC Board of Education, and comfortable in her environment. I decided to set a plan for my future, and how I would react in the singles' life again.

After the Yom Kippur holidays, and a few days spent with Ellen in Brooklyn, I drove back up to Otis and went into the living room. I sat in my favorite lounge chair in the alcove, looked around this beautiful home that I shared with a life partner, and realized that I was now going to be here all alone. It was a very unsettling feeling, and for the first time since Dorothy had passed away, I cried. It was the first time in almost fifty years that I was alone, and had no one to confide in, or talk to, or even to argue with. I was confused, and began to make an effort to get my thinking into a rational mode, and to start to make a plan for being a part of the Community again.

I rationalized that I wasn't the only man who had ever lost his wife. I even thought about what Dorothy would be saying to me if she could communicate from where she was. She would be telling me to get out there and be a part of the Community, and do the things that you did for the past fifty years. This was her unselfish nature, and she was always willing to share me with the rest of my world.

I recalled the day, when she was feeling comfortable after one series of her chemo treatments. She was sitting up in her bed, and Ellen and I were with her. She spread all of her jewelry out on the blanket, and told us how she would like for these lovely pieces to be given to family and some of her good friends. We listed about 15 items, each one earmarked for a specific person. When I made the distribution, her friends, and our relatives were very grateful for being considered, by receiving such a valuable memento from such a dearly loved person. I knew that Ellen was in 100% agreement, and was very happy to be the one who gave the gifts to our family and friends.

CHAPTER **XXX**

I must begin this new period in my life with a story about an event that happened when we were out on one of our regular Saturday Night evenings. We returned home very late, after wining and dining, and having a wonderful time with our friends. We both had a lot to drink, and Dorothy was a little unsteady. I brought her into the bedroom and had her stand against my highboy dresser. I then got her undressed by taking her clothes off inside out and put her into bed. When I got into bed, she began to cry and tell me that I didn't love her. I tried to console her and quiet her down, and said, "You know I love you, now go to sleep". Then she said, "I know that you love me, but you "NEVER TELL ME". The next morning, we resumed our regular life patterns, and the night before was just a pleasant memory. It wasn't until 10 years later that I realized how important that statement from Dorothy was and how important it would be for me not to forget in the future.

My friends in Otis were the most concerned people I had ever met and rallied to me on every occasion. I was invited to their homes to share time with them. We went out to dinners together. I wasn't being left alone and was called on to be a part of every activity. This was very good for my attitude, and I realized that I had to continue being active, if I was going to be a survivor. I never said no when I was asked to go someplace or do something with any of my friends. It gave me the confidence to be optimistic.

June 16th 2000 was the day to celebrate my 80th birthday, and I asked Ellen to come up for that weekend. She said that she had an important commitment, and would gladly come up the next weekend, and would ask the Kaufmans and Florence Siegel and her date to join us. Then she called back and told me that the other couples wanted to take me out for the birthday party, and I could bring my own date. That was a good plan, and I didn't mind the change of date.

I called my friend Gloria Rosenthal, who was a regular date for the time I was in the Berkshires, and the two of us celebrated my birthday alone. During the evening with Gloria, I asked her if she could be my date for the following Saturday, as I was being taken out for a birthday party by some of the Woodlanders. She had a previous commitment and had to decline the invitation. However, the dinner with her was a very enjoyable evening, and I went home having a little celebration, which was okay for me. Gloria was a good buddy, and we were very comfortable just being good friends. I had a good friendly relationship with her 3 daughters and their families, and this companionship was acceptable. We both did not want to have a serious relationship.

The following weekend, Ellen was with me, and Saturday night, we were picked up by the Kaufmans, and were supposed to be going to the Seven Hills Inn for the dinner party. The reservation was for 7:30, and it was about 45 minutes to the Inn. When we left our house, it was 6:45, and we were driving very slowly along route 20. I was the guest, so I couldn't complain about the fact that we were going to be late for the reservation, and as we approached a little country Inn called Belden Tavern, Jerry Kaufman pulled into their driveway and parked the car. As I got out of the car, I said to Ellen, "What the hell are we doing here; we are supposed to be going to Seven Hills". She told me to keep quiet, and not make a fuss. I was talking to myself and complaining that they were too cheap to spend money at a good restaurant. I was the first one to get to the door, and as I opened the door, all hell broke loose. The dining room lights went up, and I found all of my friends standing at tables with balloons flying and cameras clicking away. This was a total and complete surprise. I later found out that Ellen had arranged this party about six months before the event and that I was the only one in the room who didn't know it was going to happen.

The Borrelli's from Florida were there. My Masonic friends from New York were there. My friend Gloria and two of her daughters were there. All of my good friends from Otis and the Woodlands were there. Some of my Brooklyn friends were there also. Ellen had invited more than 70 people to celebrate with us. Every table had a disposable camera, and hundreds of pictures were being taken. This was the 2nd time in my life that I was totally unaware of something that was happening for me. The first time was at the final dinner at Camp Seven, at the end of my stewardship as Camp Chairman; this was the second.

There were several good will speeches from my Masonic friends, and Jerry Kaufman, who presented me with a plaque that had my name printed vertically, and there was a praiseworthy comment for each letter. We had an electric piano being played for background music, and the dinner was a most enjoyable meal. The entire evening was a complete success, and when it was all over, I asked Ellen who was paying for this party. This event was her own idea, and she planned every part of it, including paying the bill.

When I went south to Florida for the winter, I was on the auto train. This was the way I traveled for these Florida vacation periods. I drove from Otis to Washington, spent the night with my nephew Steve and his wife Karen, and then took the train to Sanford, in Florida. The drive from there to Jupiter was only 3 hours, and then I got settled. This was the yearly pattern, and it was the routing both ways. On this first trip alone, I spent several hours in the club car with a very nice couple that were married to each other, after losing their spouses. This proved to be a reinforcement of the realities with which I was to be faced. I saw in their conversations and actions that they were behaving as though they had been married for ages. They were completely in tune with each other. I never forgot that trip and never forgot our time together. This impression of their togetherness gave me the incentive to set a guideline for what I would like to find in my future plans for a new start in what would be my future life.

Many questions popped up in my mind. What do I want to do? What will I look for in a new female relationship? Where will I find such a person? What will I expect from this new friendship? What will I give to this new friendship? Many puzzling thoughts, including the most important one, which was do I want a second relationship, or to just stay single and see lots of people whenever and wherever I find the opportunity?

It didn't take me too long before I realized that I was not the type to just go out and "play the field". My personality and upbringing were very organized and structured. I had made many good friends, both male and female, during the 50 years with Dorothy, and these were solid friendships. They exist today, and I don't want to change my life habits. So, when I decided to start dating again, I adopted a format for a way to present myself to the women that I would meet or be introduced to. I realized that these women would be in the same position as I was in that they also wanted a new friendship. I had to make them comfortable and relaxed when we met for the first time, and I wanted the introduction period to be an honest one. I made it a point, early on in the conversation, to make my position very clear. This is how I explained myself, when I said:

Be my friend.

Sit at the bar with me and have a drink, and I don't care if it's ginger ale.

Dine with me and spend the evening.

I don't make any demands or expect payback.

What you want from this friendship, you can have.

What you don't want, you won't get.

Say good night, and if we don't see each other again, at least it will have been a pleasant evening.

With this type of approach, I thought that I was being very frank and honest, and the lady would be very comfortable in knowing that I wasn't planning to be aggressive.

It was just about a year after Dorothy had died that I accepted a first date. One of my neighbors in Crystal Pointe gave me the phone number of one of her co-workers, and said that she was a very nice person who had lost her husband and would be interested in meeting me. I called and made the date, and asked if I could pick her up at her apartment. She said that she would rather meet me at the restaurant. I gave her the restaurant location and agreed to meet her there. When she walked in, dressed like she was going to a wedding, I knew that she was my date. I introduced myself to her, and sat at the bar, talking, before dinner. When we got to the table, the conversation was mostly about her son, who was having a difficult time adjusting, and was going from job to job.

Most of the dinner conversation was one sided, pleasant, but very uninteresting. I was very happy to have taken the first step in going out on a date, and when I walked her to her car, I asked her why she didn't want me to pick her up. She was very honest when she said that she was very unsure of herself, and didn't want me to see where she was living. That was interesting because I learned something myself that night. Caution is a very necessary attribute.

From 1995 until 2004, I was very fortunate in that I met and dated some very interesting women. The first four or five introductions were very pleasant; however, I didn't think that I would pursue any of them. I guess it was a learning experience for me because I was being very critical, trying to figure out what continuing the friendship could lead to. I honestly didn't think that we were really compatible, and I never called for a second date.

My cousin Eleanor introduced me to a nice lady who worked with her as a real estate salesperson. She was a very nice and compatible lady, and we dated for several months. I was showing an interest in becoming closer, and I felt that she had the same inclinations. We were dating on a regular weekend basis, and I was content with that. One evening during a very pleasant dinner at a fine restaurant, we were talking about our families, and she mentioned that she had a son, a Doctor, in Chicago, and she hadn't seen him in more than three years. I was astounded and couldn't believe that this was true, and I said to her, "If I was your son in Chicago, it wouldn't be three years before I would see my mother". As soon as I finished, she jumped at me and said, "Don't talk about my children like that". I was taken aback and just remained silent.

On the way back to her house, I was mulling the incident over in my mind. When we got to the house, she said she was going to get comfortable and went into her bedroom. I was playing the piano when she came out, and she was dressed very casually, with her shirttails out, and barefoot, in her slacks. She went to the couch and stretched out like Cleopatra. I looked at her over the open piano and thought that this was no time to be playing the piano.

We were together, on the couch, and started smooching. It was getting to be very emotional, and then I backed off. I got up off the couch, and told her that I wasn't feeling right, and that I was going home.

While I was driving home, I realized that this friendship would have some serious complications. I am family oriented, and matching up with a person who has family difficulties would not work for me. I was looking for a family compatibility relationship, and I could see that this wasn't going in that direction. I realized that if I took her to bed, I would be making a commitment, and I wasn't comfortable with that thought. And I didn't want her to think I was just another user. When I called her and explained that I didn't think we could be more than just friends, we realized that it wouldn't work that way either. I didn't call her again.

I decided to be more aware of the fact that I wanted a relationship that would meld with my ideas of what a new relationship should mean. I had a family oriented relationship for almost fifty years, and I wanted to find that again.

My good friend Ira Adler introduced me to a lady who was his girlfriend's neighbor in Boca Raton. We went out on a double date, and I found her to be a very nice companion. We dated for a few weeks, and then I went back up to Otis for the summer. This lady had a summer home in upstate New York and drove a car. I invited her to spend a few days with me in Otis, and she accepted. When the summer was over, and I went south for the winter, she did also, and we continued the relationship in Florida. We were seeing each other for a few months, with the understanding that we didn't want any commitment. We did many things together, but most of them hinged around her friends and her interests, which was costume making for the show people in her Community. This activity was very time consuming, and I didn't want to discourage her from that activity. I was feeling that my position was a second place interest. I had to expect that and decided to sever the relationship. No regrets on either part, and no harm done because I had an occasion to meet her one day in a restaurant where I was with another lady, and she came over and gave me a hug and said hello. I introduced her to my companions and then she left.

My next attempt at a relationship started with an introduction to a lady from a nearby town in Massachusetts. On our first dinner date, we had a very lengthy conversation over a bottle of wine, which we ordered with dinner. She was not interested in a relationship, but would be glad to be a friend. I felt comfortable with that, and a good friendship was started.

This friendship lasted for several years, and we traveled together on several interesting trips. We went to Australia for a visit to my friends down under. The next year we spent time in Mexico at a hotel in Cancun. She visited me in Florida during the winter, and I was comfortable with her family when I visited with them. This friendship had been keeping me busy socially, and I was very contented. She was a good traveling partner, and a willing dinner partner. We had no conflict of personalities. The ground rules were established and I was comfortable with them. She always said that I needed someone better than she was because I was a very nice man, and even her children and grandchildren liked me.

One of my Masonic friends, Dave Kimmel, persuaded me to join his local Shrine organization and his mariners club. He was going to be the incoming Commodore and he wanted me to be on his team. I knew that they were interested in the Children's Hospital in Tampa, and that they were driving children from our area to the hospital for their treatments. When I joined this group, I found out that I was the only member who didn't own a boat. I became a member of the "roadrunners", which was the group of Shriners who drove the vans to the Hospital from Palm Beach Gardens. We picked up the patients at 5:30 AM and drove the 200miles to Tampa. We waited in the recreation hall until their treatments were concluded, and then drove them back to our Temple, where their parents picked them up again.

My first trip to the Shriners's hospital convinced me that this was going to be a most worthy effort, and I was going to devote my efforts to this worthy project. I was in the recreation hall, waiting for the kids to be finished with their treatments, when I saw this little five year old girl. She was a very pretty child, with a Buster Brown haircut, and as she walked towards me, I saw that she was holding a coke can in her arms because she had no hands. Her arms were clamped around the can in a viselike grip. I waved to her, and she responded by putting the can down on a table, and she waved back. Then she picked up the can again and kept walking with her friends. That was the clincher, and I was hooked. This volunteer driving was going to be a regular part of my weekly activities.

As I got more involved with the Mariners, I began to think about how I could fundraise for this worthy charity. It didn't take more than the next year, and I was persuaded to step into the Commodore's station. As part of my administrative plans I started to formulate a fund raising project, which is a letter to be sent to friends of the Shrine membership, asking them to be generous and contribute to our Hospital Transportation Fund. I feel that the Shriners have been very active themselves, and I didn't want to impose any additional financial burden on them. Asking them for names and addresses would be more advantageous for my project, and I am soliciting the 1400 members to send me names. This project is working, and at this writing, the contributions received have been in excess of four thousand dollars. This letter writing campaign will be an ongoing project. Working for children has been a very regular part of my life, and I hope to continue in this most important work.

CHAPTER XXXI

When I returned to Florida in 2004, I decided to sign up for membership in a dating club. I realized that friendships were okay, but I really wanted someone permanent in my life again. I had several nice female companions for dinner dates in Florida, and these women were part of our party nights in the Community, as my date. I was never lonesome, but I was getting lonely, and I wanted someone in my life again.

The dating club sent me a few names of women in the club, and a picture of each one. I decided to give it a try, and made a few phone calls. In my first two attempts, I met two ladies who were totally interested in their agendas, and dating was a secondary interest. These dates were very unsatisfactory, and I never called either one again.

My third introduction was to a lady named Sharry Israel. I had told the Agency that I was seventy- five years old, and wanted to meet a woman a little younger. I told the agency that I wanted to meet her, and the following day, the Agency called me and said that Ms. Israel didn't want to go out with me because I was too old for her. I told the Agency person to call her and tell her that I wanted to take her out for lunch, and she could pick the restaurant. If she wasn't happy with the date, she wouldn't have to count it as one of her recommended dates. The following day, I got the okay to call her, and I made a date for lunch.

It was March 8, 2004 that I met Sharry Israel. She had picked Richard's restaurant in Boynton Beach for our lunch date, and we met in the entry room. First impressions were very acceptable, and when we were at the table, I felt very comfortable and relaxed. This lady was very neatly dressed and very pleasant to look at and completely at ease. As the luncheon progressed, the conversation became very casual, and I think I did most of the talking because she was not too talkative. I did think that she was comfortable and was enjoying the time together. We shared some personal information regarding our past lives, and what it was like to be alone. I told her what my intention was, and that I wanted to have a friendship that could be developed. I was very pleased to have the opportunity to be in her company. When we left for our cars, I asked her if she would mind if I called her again. I said that I would like to see her again. She agreed, and we said goodbye in the parking lot.

During the following week, Sharry and I had several phone conversations, and they were very enjoyable. She mentioned that she was planning on selling her Condo and buying a new home in a community in Lake Worth called Bellaggio. We made another date for lunch, and I picked her up at her Condo. Her apartment was very well decorated and comfortable layout. The walls were covered with interesting paintings, most of which were Israeli oriented.

We were having a very interesting conversation during lunch, and I casually mentioned that "when I graduated from College in 1941", Sharry interrupted and said, "Wait a minute, I was born in 1941. You can't be seventy five". Then I said, "Well I lied a little in my resume". I don't think that it was too damaging, but now all of the cards were open and on the table. We had several more dates, and then Sharry mentioned that she wanted me to meet one of her good friends. This was not good news for me because I was getting the impression that she and I were getting comfortable with this friendship. I wasn't anxious to be handed off to anyone else. I began to realize that the age difference was putting up a barrier, and I had to overcome that handicap.

Sharry told me that she had contracted for her new house and that she couldn't take occupancy until the end of the summer. She had plans to move into her Aunt's Condo in Century Village while they were up north in New Jersey. Then she learned that she wouldn't be allowed to stay there because she was not a blood relative. I told her it wasn't a problem because she could stay in my spare bedroom after she had to leave her apartment. There would be all the privacy she would need. My home had two bedrooms with two bathrooms, and each was on the other end of the house. This was an acceptable proposal, and Sharry could finalize her plans for closing on the sale of the Condo.

I told Ellen that I was getting serious in my relationship with Sharry, and that I wanted to make her a part of my future life. Ellen had met Sharry several times prior to that day, and then said "she's a keeper". I asked her why she never said anything about the other women that I dated, she responded, " I don't have to like your friends, you do". I knew that Ellen would be a friend and part of our life. And, as times have progressed, she has shown her friendship in many ways.

Our relationship was beginning to be very comfortable together, and I was a happy man again. We were out for dinner one evening, and ran into her friend Eadie, who was there with a few of her women friends. Then she told me that Eadie was the woman she wanted me to meet. Eadie is a very nice person, and we have been out with her several times. When I met Sharry, I didn't want to meet any other women. I honestly felt that I could be happy with my relationship with her, and I would have to make her feel the same about me.

One evening we got back to Sharry's apartment after a nice dinner out, and we were sitting on the couch. I said it was getting late, and I should head for home. Sharry said, why don't you sleep over? I said, "I didn't have any pajamas", and she said, "Sleep in your underwear". I agreed, and we continued talking.

I knew that there were two bedrooms, and I headed to the back of the apartment to get ready for bed. When I passed her bedroom, I saw that both sides of the blanket were turned down. This was a very pleasant surprise, and one which I was not expecting. I must admit that I was very happy knowing that I had been wishing for this day. I was never an aggressive person, and I would not make any unwanted moves. In this situation, this is an invitation that I would never refuse. In reality, it was the invitation that I was hoping for since we first met.

When I got into bed, I had a very awkward feeling, and I had my slacks on. I guess that I was very unsure of what was happening. It was a very long time since I was in this position, and I really was a bit nervous. Sharry said it was ok to take my slacks off and sleep in my shorts. I got into bed, turned to Sharry, and with the first kiss, I knew that this is where I wanted to be. It was a wonderful feeling, and I realized that I was in love again. I never thought that it would happen to me, but I was lucky. I found someone to love again.

Meeting Sharry was the best thing that could have happened for me. After Dorothy died, I had an attitude that I would just coast through the years, and do whatever appealed to me. I had made very good female friendships and could always find a nice companion to join me for an evening dinner or entertainment. I was never lonesome, and I was back in the swim. I kept myself busy with the daily activities and interests that I had been used to. I didn't have to answer to anyone, and could do as I pleased. My daily activities filled the days, and my social activities filled the evenings. My weight jumped from 165 pounds to 197 pounds. I was never lonesome, but I was very lonely. When I went home after one of my evenings out and turned the computer on, I played bridge with some of my friends on the west coast. I kept my dates out as late as I could because I knew that I was going home alone. No hits, no runs and no errors was the way I treated my lady friends. I wanted them to be comfortable and relaxed.

The next two months were very enjoyable and exciting. Sharry and I moved back and forth, and we spent the night wherever we were for that evening. Some of our dates were with my friends in Palm Beach Gardens, and other dates were with the Boynton friends. My bedroom in Crystal Pointe had twin beds on a double headboard, and one of us was always falling into the crack between the beds. I solved the problem and bought a king size mattress and box spring, and the crack disappeared.

Commuting back and forth was not the best choice for our relationship, and Sharry asked me if I would want to move into her new house with her. I thought about it for a short while, and then

I agreed. It would be the best arrangement. In the meantime, I brought some of my clothing down to the new house because it would be more convenient. Every time we left Crystal Pointe for the night in Lake Worth, I brought more of my personal effects down with us.

Living as a couple was very comforting. I was back in an environment for which I was longing. I wanted to be part of Sharry's life, and I was committed to making our new relationship a successful partnership. I felt that her feelings towards me were the same because I knew that I wanted her for me as much as she wanted me for her. I was certain that I could make this new partnership succeed. I remembered how I reacted when I saw other friends in a similar situation and saw a different attitude. Our relationship was fated to be a successful one because we both felt exactly the same. I knew, from past experience, that being honest and truthful has its own rewards. I wanted to share our lives together and that included living expenses.

We were planning on my compensating Sharry for some of her homeowner expenses, but soon after, decided to share the expenses in a very simple manner. Sharry was to take care of the inside, and I was going to take care of the outside. This is her home, and she is responsible for her expenses. I take care of the outside, which includes travel and entertainment and whatever comes up on a daily basis.

I couldn't appreciate other friendships, where each of the people paid their share of the dinner expenses. I didn't appreciate comments like, it's not my problem, "it's hers"; or "she pays and I pay". I always believed that a partnership is exactly what it means. Everything in a relationship should be shared, and that's what makes for a solid bond. I learned that as a child, and I believe that still holds true. I have formed a bond that gives me the confidence to believe that it will be a very rewarding relationship.

I inherited Sharry's family with open arms. She has become a friend to my daughter Ellen, who lives in the same community. When Ellen decided to move to Florida after she retired, I helped her decide when she chose to buy a home in Bellaggio. I never connected the coincidence until I came to Bellaggio for the first time. Ellen bought an

Ansca Home, and Sharry bought a Levitt home. The houses are directly across the main road in the Community.

Living under the same roof had put me in a very comfortable state of mind, and I began to feel a warmth that had been missing since Dorothy had passed away. Even though I knew that I didn't own any part of the house, I knew that I belonged here, and I had a comfortable glow because Sharry and I were so happy together. There is a great deal of humor in our relationship, and that makes it all the more exciting. I often make a comment and ask Sharry, "When are we going to have an argument"? She laughs, and then we change the subject. We don't' even worry about who takes out the trash on Wednesday and Saturday. It just happens, just like many other daily tasks. I believe that we both know the way to act to have a very happy and compatible relationship. I guess it can be explained in a few simple words. "Give and you shall receive" is a parable handed down from the ages. We practice that tenet, and sharing common interests and reponsibilities as a team makes for a very happy relationship.

Our social life includes a group called the Midwest Club, which is where Sharry hails from originally. I became an honorary member, and we travel with this group on vacation excursions. Some of these people have become my friends, and that has been another plus for me. I realized that my joining with Sharry, in her environment, would make it necessary for me to adapt. It wasn't difficult because these Midwesterners are just as friendly as the friends I already have. We travel to my friends on occasion, and all's well. Sharry has been accepted with open arms wherever I take her, and I have been accepted equally as well where she takes me.

My relationship with Sharry has given me a second family, and I am very comfortable in making these new family connections. When I went to visit her mother for the first time, we had a very pleasant Sunday afternoon and dinner. Ruth Polen is a very lovely lady, who is disabled, and needs a walker to assist her when she moves around. We spend almost every Sunday with "Mom" and take her to an afternoon movie, and then out to dinner. Sharry's brother, Mark and his wife, Barbara, are usually part of this afternoon activity. My daughter Ellen shares the same feelings as I, and has been welcomed into the new family as well.

We moved into our new home in August 2004, and about a week later, we left for a week in Branson, Missouri, where we spent a week going to shows every evening. This area is the focal point for entertainment showcasing in the entire country. There are about thirty five different theatres in a few square miles, and the attractions are designed for every interest. Visitors from all walks of life come there, and the facilities were capable of accommodating the needs of every pocket. We had a lovely time and planned on leaving for home on Saturday. Hurricane Francis had hit Florida, and we were delayed for two days. When we got home, there was no damage to the house, and we settled back in.

Sharry and I traveled to New Hampshire in October 2004, for her annual visit to her daughter, Jenny, her husband, Daryn and the three grandchildren. Ben was nine, Nathan was five, and Isabel was not quite two. This was my first connection with her daughter and her family. I was very delighted to be accepted as a new member of their family. I knew that I wasn't a grandfather, but now I could think that I was. Ellen has no children, and now I can lay claim to having "younguns" to cherish and watch grow up. It was a very comfortable feeling to have Daryn tell me that his kids look at me as the grandfather they never had.

Most of my adult life included work and philanthropies that looked after children, and I was always buying little gadgets and gifts to give to "other people's grandchildren". Now I have inherited my own, and I haven't stopped accumulating "stuff" to send or bring to them. This is one of my greatest pleasures. I love taking pictures of people's faces, but seeing these little faces light up when our gifts arrive is worth all the money in the world. I look forward to every opportunity to visit with them.

Our next trip in May of 2005 was a tour of Italy with the Perrillo Travel Company. Our first stop was Lugano, in Switzerland, and we were sightseeing the shops that were not open. It was some kind of Swiss holiday, and the only shop open was a jewelry store. While Sharry was touring the shop with some of the other people, I was looking at rings on the outside window display. I saw some rings in the window that were interesting, and I brought Sharry out to take a look at what I was looking at. When she came out, I pointed to the rings I was interested in, and asked her if she wanted to pick one of them for herself. She looked at the rings, which were wedding bands, and asked me why. Then, I asked her to marry me. I had been thinking about that decision for weeks, and when this opportunity came up, I thought it would be a very appropriate time. I knew from the beginning of our relationship that I wanted to make it permanent and be married again. We went into the shop, and the salesperson took the ring from the showcase, and when Sharry put it on her finger, it was a perfect fit. When we boarded the bus, and were riding back to our hotel, Sharry said that she would marry me. Our fellow passengers were very happy to hear the news, and congratulations were coming to us from all of the travelers. I asked the tour guide if he could arrange for a wedding, and he told me that it takes four days for the paper work in Italy, and the bus wasn't going to wait. I was ecstatic and as happy as could be. This was a very happy day, and I knew that the rest of the trip would be sensational. The next two weeks proved to be as we expected, and every city we visited was full of beautiful sites and attractions. Our tour guide was excellent, and he made our trip an experience worth remembering.

Our last dinner in Rome was in an old palace, and the service and food was excellent. I could compare it with the finest ever in New York. Wine poured like water, music was delightful, and our group was having a marvelous time. I had my digital camera and was taking pictures of everyone at each table in our group. There must have been about 150 exposures of the trip that were ready to be developed. I had already printed about 100 pictures while we were in Verona. I was resting at a fountain while the tour was walking through the town. When our group left the Palace, and were about to get on our bus, I realized that I had left my camera on the banquet table. I ran back inside and found the table had been cleared. When I asked the staff if anyone found a camera on our table, no one could tell me anything. The camera was gone, and the last two days of photos went with it. There was some benefit later on, when one of our tour friends sent me some of their pictures that they had taken. On the upside, this evening was one of the most memorable of the entire tour. We had been treated like Royalty.

The two weeks in Italy with the Perrillo tour were very interesting, and we learned a great deal about the "old culture" in the museums and palaces that we visited. Visiting the "Romeo and Juliet" home in Verona, and seeing the photo shots being taken of tourist couples standing on the same balcony was memorable. Riding in a gondola in Venice, with a troubador singing Italian love songs, was romantic. We even had champagne to drink as we floated around the canals. The museums in Florence were crowded, and visiting the "David" and " Moses" sculptures was an overwhelming experience. It was truly a very enlightening trip, and one which will be long remembered.

On the flight back from Rome to Miami, we were discussing future plans, and Sharry told me that she was planning on a special birthday for me, and she had arranged for an 85th birthday party. Sharry and Ellen had a meeting and put a guest list together. Sharry had chosen Brooks Restaurant, one of the better places in South Florida. All of her family was invited, and my friends and family that were here were to be part of the celebration. This was the first time that all of our friends and families were together in the same place. Sharry was the MC and told excerpts of my past life, which surprised me, as she told tidbits from my early childhood until the time that I met her. I never knew that she had such a retentive memory because she was able to recall all of these events on different occasions when we were retelling our past lives, and the incidents were stored in her memory. When she had finished her remarks, she introduced Ellen to her family and asked her to speak.

When Ellen got up to speak, I was "kvelling" because I knew that she was going to make me appear to be a King. All I can write now is to quote her remarks, as I have done earlier in this story.

"In what seems just a few years ago, some of you were at my Dad's 80th birthday party, where lots of people spoke about what a great guy he is. Well, he still is a great guy, but our attention span (if not our memories), are shorter, so I will be exceedingly brief. "My dad has many admirable qualities. Since all of you here are either relatives who know him longer, and more objectively than I, or people who have chosen to be long time friends, you can all name some of those qualities".

"Those of you who know me well, know that I believe you should strive to learn at least one new thing a day, and I believe that we can learn something from everyone. Since our parents are our first teachers, I've been watching my dad for all of my years".

"AND, some of the things that I have already learned from him are:

If you involve yourself in the lives of others, you will have REALLY GOOD FRIENDS.

Our main job in life is to work on making the world a better place.

The true value of money is in the good that it can do; otherwise it is just paper.

And, like Dad's Mom always said, if you give charitably, when you put your hand back in your pocket, there will always be more there".

Some of the things I'd like to learn from him are:

How to take things as they are and not analyze them.

How to believe that all things will work out.

How to see the best in other people.

Hopefully, we'll all have many more years of teaching and learning ahead of us, at his 90th birthday party. I'll be able to list a few more things that I have mastered, and a few more yet to learn. "Thanks Dad, for being a great role model".

There wasn't much that I could add to all of the prior accolades, so I thanked everyone for coming, and we enjoyed a great luncheon, which ended with fabulous desserts.

This was a very memorable day, and having both of my favorite women sharing the day with me at the same time made me the happiest man on earth.

It was soon after the birthday party that Sharry and I discussed a wedding date. Sharry was wearing the ring that I bought in

Lugano, Switzerland, and I wanted to make it official. We agreed on August 27th and arranged for the ceremony to be held at home.

Sharry's immediate family and a few of her close friends were invited. I invited Ellen and some of my close friends, and a few cousins who live in the area. It was a beautiful ceremony, and we all went out for dinner at a local restaurant to celebrate the occasion. Now, my life was complete again. I was happily married to a lovely and loving woman, who was very loved by me, and I was looking forward to a happy future.

For a wedding present, I would be taking Sharry to visit some dear friends in Sydney, and tour New Zealand and the Outback for four weeks. We left for Aukland, New Zealand at the end of October, and picked up the Tauck tour when we arrived in Aukland. We spent a week touring New Zealand in a private tour jet, and tour bus, and were treated to the best scenery and sites imaginable. Our accommodations were first class in every location, and I took many photos, which will fill up an album.

When we flew to Sydney, we met Jan and Noel at the airport, and they took us to Noel's home, where we were to stay for the time in Sydney. This was a reunion for me, and a first meeting for Sharry. This was my fourth trip to visit with Jan, and Sharry was coming as my new bride. Needless to say, the warmth and affection that was extended to us both was beautiful, and we felt completely at home. We spent an evening with some of Jan's children during this short stay, and many reminiscences were shared.

We flew to Ayres Rock and saw one of the "Wonders of the World", then flew to Darwin, to have dinner with Sharry's cousin, who was living there. We visited a replica of an Opal mine, and did all the things that tourists do on such a trip. I wanted Sharry to see all of these wonders, and to meet my special friend Jan, who has been a friend since 1942. This "Aussie" friendship has lasted more than sixty four years.

The flight home to Miami was long and tiring. The recollections of all the good that we saw and did were worth the trip. This tour to New Zealand and Australia should be on every tourist's list of places to go to and see the sights. We rested for about a week, and then embarked on a four day cruise with some of Sharry's friends from Coral Lakes, and rested some more. After doing a great deal of traveling in 2005, we decided to slow down and spend a quiet New Year's Eve at home.

We started 2006 with a super 90th birthday party for Sharry's mom, Ruth, and returned to Brooks Restaurant for the event. It was a fabulous party, and cousins of the honoree were with her to help in the celebration. We were thirty-four people, and believe it or not, there were four people at the party who were older than the honoree.

Now that we are completely rested up, we have plans for future travel in 2006.

Our first trip, in the middle of April was to visit with Jenny and Daryn and the three grandkids, in New Hampshire. The next trip was the end of April, when we went to Austin, Texas for a wedding, and then on to Las Vegas to visit a few of my friends, and then on to San Bernadino in California, to see some of Sharry's friends. At the end of July, we will leave for England, Ireland, Scotland and Wales, for a two week tour of the sites.

We plan to make another trip to Jenny and her family in October, which will be our last trip for 2006, and an annual trip for the future. We will be detouring to New York for a testimonial dinner, on the trip home from New Hampshire, where I will be speaking in honor of one of my friends who will be the Masonic District Deputy from my Lodge in New York.

On June 16, 2006 we celebrated my 86th birthday. And so it goes.

TO BE CONTINUED...........................

EPILOGUE

Early in this story, I referred to a comment from my father-in-law, when he replied to his daughter, my wife Dorothy, when she complained to him about my being out almost every night in the week. His answer was simple, and he told her not to worry. He told her that I was young and ambitious, and wanted to be an activist in Community activities. He also said that there would come a time when I would settle down and become a family man.

I was a Basketball referee and a member of the Kings County Association of Referees.

I was and still am an active Mason and Shriner.

I was a Congregation President and helped build a new Synagogue

I was an active member of our Political Club in Brooklyn and helped the advancement of people in our Community, such as Senator Charles Schumer. I didn't seek any office.

I was Master of my Lodge and District Deputy Grand Master of Grand Lodge of N.Y.

I was the Camp Chairman of Masonic Camp Seven for six years and supervised the vacation of 600 little girls each summer.

I was the President of my Community Home Owner Association in Florida.

I am still active in fund raising for children's causes.

When I returned from the Army in 1945, I was 25 years old, and I dedicated myself to working and sharing myself wherever I could be useful. I also realized that I was extending myself to the fullest, and somewhere I would have some shortcomings. My almost fifty years with my wife Dorothy and Ellen were good years, and my family prospered. My wife, Dorothy, will always be in my memory, and I know that she always supported everything that I did. I loved her, as she loved me, and will never forget our years together. My daughter Ellen is a friend, and is perfectly happy with my new life with my beautiful and loving wife, Sharry. I have everything that a man could wish for.

There are many places and things that I have still not seen and done. I still have the desire to be productive and contribute to this wonderful life that I am privileged to share with my family and friends. I will always believe that this is "ONE WORLD WITH ONE PEOPLE".

My priorities have changed. This new life will see me focusing my interests to living and sharing my future years with my loving wife Sharry and my wonderful daughter Ellen.